Justin Huffman takes the   d
helps us to view them a   y
that both fascinates us ¿   k
that focuses attention on Jesus and says, 'Behold your God!'

JOEL R. BEEKE
President, Puritan Reformed Theological Seminary,
Grand Rapids, Michigan

What captures your wonder? What gets you to pause in your busyness and be filled with awe? Huffman's book *Behold* is an invitation to wonder as he takes us on a journey through places in the New Testament where the text urges us to 'Behold.' This word tells us to stop and take notice. It is a word which points to the all glorious and the awesome—to the wondrous person and work of Jesus Christ. Dear reader, as you read *Behold* may your heart be wonderstruck at the glories of who Christ is and what He has done.

CHRISTINA FOX
Author of *A Holy Fear: Trading Lesser Fears for the Fear of the Lord*

'We are far too easily pleased,' said C.S. Lewis in comparing the mundane activities we find satisfaction in when far greater joy is within grasp. In the fast-paced world in which we live, it's far too easy to lose oneself in the ordinaries of life and forget the glory and wonder of Christ who has fashioned all things. *Behold* reorients our minds and hearts away from the small pleasures to the grand wonders of living in a world ruled by God's sovereign hand. Refresh yourself in the streams of this thoroughly biblical worldview, that when adopted, will change everything.

DUSTIN BENGE
Provost and professor, Union School of Theology, Bridgend, Wales

Sometimes we yawn at God's truths, not because His truths are dull but because our hearts are. In this book, Justin Huffman helps us recapture the beauty and the glory of God and His gospel. If you, like me, are in danger of taking God's truth for granted, *Behold* will help to reawaken your wonder and worship.

DARRYL DASH
Pastor of Liberty Grace Church, Toronto
Author of *8 Habits for Growth: A Simple Guide to Becoming More like Christ*

Justin Huffman helps us challenge what we truly love, what we spend our time beholding. In a world full of distractions and digital delights, this is a timely call to gaze at the face of Jesus and bask in His glory. *Behold* provides a corrective lens for us to see that there is more to life and invites us to satisfy our deep soul-hunger by feasting on Jesus, the Son of God. But we're not left there to gorge on glory while the world starves. We must respond in wonder and worship, and by taking the good news to a fatally sick world so they can behold Jesus too.

JOEL MORRIS
Executive Director, Union School of Theology, Bridgend, Wales

JUSTIN O.
HUFFMAN

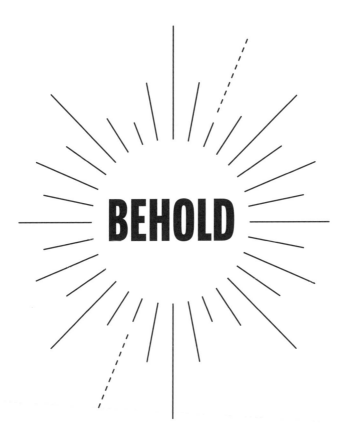

BEHOLD

AN
INVITATION TO
WONDER

Copyright © Justin O. Huffman 2021

paperback ISBN 978-1-5271-0723-6
ebook ISBN 978-1-5271-0820-2

10 9 8 7 6 5 4 3 2 1

Published in 2021
by
Christian Focus Publications, Ltd.
Geanies House, Fearn,
Ross-shire, IV20 1TW, Scotland.
www.christianfocus.com

Cover design by Tom Barnard

Printed and bound by
Bell & Bain, Glasgow

MIX
Paper from
responsible sources
FSC® C007785

CONTENTS

To Kurt Strassner, Hannah Weaver, and Rebecca Huffman—
you each played a crucial role in bringing this book to
fruition. Thank you!

INTRODUCTION

The world will never starve for want of wonders; but only for want of wonder.
—G.K. Chesterton

Most of the world is starving. And it seems citizens of economically prosperous nations are starving the most. We are starving for want of wonder. We may be briefly entertained by the special effects in the latest blockbuster movie. We may be periodically impressed with the athletic skills of our favorite sports team. We may be temporarily delighted by a vacation with our family. On an ongoing basis, however, in what we perceive to be the desert wasteland of daily life and regular responsibilities, we are often starving because we lack a basic sense of wonder.

Our souls hunger for more. We instinctively feel there must be more to life than merely waiting for the next big movie to be released, or the next sport season to come back around, or the next holiday to arrive on the calendar. We long to be truly in awe. We long so much for it, in fact, that many of us have taken to using the word 'awesome' to describe things or events that in reality barely register as interesting. So we seek to satisfy our soul-hunger by coming up with grander schemes for inspiring ourselves. We compile a 'bucket list' of things we want to do before we die as if ticking off such to-do items as traveling to another country or riding in a hot air balloon will somehow give our life additional spark or more meaning.

All the while, true wonders abound. They abound in the natural world, and they super-abound in the supernatural realm.

God's Wonderful World

The entire creation is commanded, in Psalm 148, to praise the Lord—from dragons to judges, from snow to snowy-haired men. We are reminded by David in another song that creation is actually doing just that: 'The heavens declare the glory of God, and the sky above proclaims his handiwork' (Ps. 19:1). David sings again, in Psalm 8, 'O LORD, our Lord, how majestic is your name in all the earth!'

It is a worthwhile and encouraging habit to take the time to hear what the creation is saying about our God! The Grand Canyon and oceans declare His bigness and majesty. The atoms and breezes proclaim His invisible power and wisdom. Symphonies and sea slugs reflect His beauty and ingenuity.

It seems God has tucked away bits and pieces of His glory into every corner of His creation. Every single section of the universe is in some way pointing us to its Maker.

Meanwhile, we often wake up, get dressed, feed the kids, stumble out the door, and make our way to our first appointment of the day without so much as a glance at God's glory or a thought about His majesty. We barely notice the resplendent sunrise; we are not amazed by the physics of raindrops; we do not even consider the multi-faceted marvel that is our human body. The sounds of birds chirping, of leaves rustling, of children laughing all fall on ears that are deaf to God's glory reflected in His creation. Instead, we find ourselves—on a good day—wrestling with boredom. On a bad day, we end the day exhausted and depressed.

We are starving for wonder. Our souls are shriveling because they were made to feed on truly awesome realities and instead we are tossing them the crumbs of dreary escapism.

God's Super-Abounding Glory

God's entire creation is constantly—day and night—pointing us to the majesty of its Maker. However, even the wonders of God's natural world pale in comparison to the glory of what God has and is doing to accomplish His great plan of redemption. Solar systems and sand storms are, ultimately, merely reminders of their Creator. But Jesus is God's own Son. Jesus is the very 'radiance of the glory of God and the exact imprint of his nature, and he upholds the universe by the word of his power' (Heb. 1:3). We could spend a lifetime studying the brilliance of corneas or constellations and, in the end, we still would not have discovered the secret to life after death. Yet even the feeblest faith in Jesus as Savior is guaranteed to transform our lives here and now, and then throw open the gates to an eternity with God in heaven.

In the end, what our souls are starving for is not merely to be awed, but to discover something or someone that is truly, permanently, and altogether awesome. This is why pastor and author David Platt asserts that 'people today are not starved for great music. They're not starved for entertaining speeches. People today are starved for the greatness of God.'[1] We will forever hunger for more until we discover—or rediscover— the greatness of God.

This is no surprise to God. He is the one who made us immortal in the first place. And God knows that He alone is the food that will satisfy our eternal souls. This is why He gave us not only His Son Jesus, but also His Word the Bible. The Bible is the great story of the greatness of God.

The Bible purposefully sets in front of us rock-solid and mind-blowing reasons to believe in, delight in, and find our confidence in the God of the Bible. Yet we can so easily rush through the Bible like we rush through our day, ignoring the wonder of all that is taking place in front of our eyes. We get used to the often-told narratives, so we are no longer amazed when we read that God created the entire cosmos with just His words. We are not surprised when we read Isaiah's description of the Messiah hundreds of years before Jesus' birth. And we are not astonished when Jesus rises from the dead, ascends into heaven, and promises to return again. We can even be untouched to hear Jesus' anguished cry on the cross, 'My

1   As quoted by Tony Reinke: https://twitter.com/TonyReinke/status/1169060442490015744.

God, my God, why have you forsaken me?' and therefore lack the curiosity to search the Scriptures for the answer to Jesus' question.

Behold!

God knows both our need and His sufficiency to meet it. Yet God also knows our propensity, as humans, to grow calloused to the glory that surrounds us every day and confronts us every time we open the Bible. It is for this reason that God tells us, over and over again, to focus our starving souls on the superb reality of who He is, what He is doing, and what He promises to do for all who trust in Him. God invites us to pause within the pages of Scripture, to consider what we are reading, and thereby to feed on His majesty. And God's invitation to glory in Him is nowhere more explicit than in the repeated command to 'Behold.'

The command to 'Behold' appears over 200 times in the New Testament, many times quoting the over 900 times that the equivalent term is used in the Old Testament. Each time this imperative is used to call our attention as readers to what is being said or seen or done.

Behold. It is a potent word, inviting us to slow from our hurried pace in order to gaze at what God has put before us in His Word. It is meant to make us linger, consider, and be amazed by the subject matter being described. Not every use of the command to 'Behold' is related to a positive event, because sometimes there are striking acts of wrong-doing as well. Yet whenever we are instructed to 'Behold' godly people or events, we can be sure this occasion is worth our notice and consideration. When we come across such constantly recurring opportunities in Scripture, each time we should hear God saying to us, 'Pay careful attention to what follows. This is important!' Or as we might say to a friend, 'Listen to this!' The exhortation to 'Behold' is like an ancient version of our exclamation mark, or bold italics, or even highlighting. It is an invitation to glory. It is a pointer for starving people to the very real wonders that ought to delight our souls.

When we read the word *behold* we should expect whatever follows to be very special. It is significant. It is crucial for us to pay attention. It is the food for which we have been starving.

God's Gracious Invitation

I well remember the first time I visited Niagara Falls. I was afraid I might be disappointed, that the Falls might not be that remarkable after all. How wrong I was! Standing next to Niagara means having all your everyday concepts of power and splendor recalibrated in an instant. Or at least it meant that for me, and for everyone else on the *Maiden of the Mist*. Except one. I could not help but notice that the only person not fascinated by the Falls was our tour guide. He was actually the opposite, evidently and completely unimpressed to be so near Niagara Falls in all its magnificence. He had seen the Falls so many times he had grown deaf to its roar, blind to its beauty, calloused to its glory. While the rest of us couldn't get enough of the Falls, our tour guide was noticeably bored with the entire event.

Similarly, as we are regularly rubbing shoulders with the grandeur of God's creation, or even with the truth claims of Scripture, we become numb if we are not careful. We are starving, not for lack of wonders, but for lack of wonder. But the Bible serves as a tour guide that is itself still in awe of the greatness of what it is describing for us. The Bible cries out to us over and over again, 'Behold!' It is an invitation to glory, whether for the first time or for the thousandth time in your decades-long walk of faith.

In this book, then, we want to consider some of these truths, some of these occasions, some of these people that the Bible tells us specifically to 'Behold.' And as we do, we can be sure that our want of wonder will finally be supplied. We will not only be awestruck; we will be enjoying the One who is truly, permanently, and altogether awesome.

1 IMMANUEL, GOD WITH US

God became man. Nothing in fiction is so fantastic as this truth of the incarnation.
—J.I. Packer

There are some things, the Bible writers remind us, that are simply worth taking a long and careful look at. And the birth of Jesus Christ is certainly one of them.

Not surprisingly, then, the New Testament opens with more than *ten occurrences* of the command to 'Behold' as the story of Christ's birth is narrated. We are called to consider the uniqueness, the majesty, the very miracle of this pivotal event of all history: '*Behold,* the virgin shall conceive and bear a son, and they shall call his name Immanuel (which means, God with us)' (Matt. 1:23).

Look! Listen! Consider the marvelous realities that attended the coming of the Christ. Behold.

The Prophesied Coming of Christ

We are called to notice, first of all, how purposeful the coming of Christ was. Mark opens his gospel by telling us that it is not actually *his* gospel: it is the gospel of Jesus Christ. Mark writes,

> The beginning of the gospel of Jesus Christ, the Son of God. As it is written in Isaiah the prophet, '*Behold,* I send my messenger before your face, who will prepare your way, the voice of one crying in the wilderness: "Prepare the way of the Lord, make his paths straight"' (Mark 1:1-3).

This prophecy is speaking specifically of John the Baptist who would come as a precursor to the Messiah, preaching repentance and pointing others to him. But ultimately the prophecy is drawing attention—not to the messenger, not to the precursor, but—to the event itself. Our focus is drawn to the one whom the messenger is heralding, whom the emissary is ushering in. And this herald for the Messiah was prophesied 700 years beforehand by Isaiah, as Mark reminds us.

In fact, Isaiah was not alone in foretelling this forerunner to the Messiah. Malachi also purposefully pointed us to him, saying, '*Behold,* I send my messenger, and he will prepare the way before me. And the Lord whom you seek will suddenly come to his temple; and the messenger of the covenant in whom you delight, *behold,* he is coming, says the Lord of hosts' (Mal. 3:1).

This is just a sampling of the many reminders from Scripture that the coming of the Christ was planned. It was foretold. It was purposed long beforehand. In fact, it was purposed by the Christ Himself. Did you notice who is speaking in the first person through Malachi's prophecy? '*I* will send *my* messenger, and he will prepare the way before *me*.' This is God Himself saying, in effect, 'I myself will prepare a messenger to go before me when I, the Lord, come to you—and it will be something to behold.'

Jesus is not the great jack-in-the-box of history, springing up suddenly—maybe even unpleasantly—out of nowhere as an utterly unexpected prophet or teacher or miracle man. Jesus' birth was planned before the world began! It was prophesied hundreds of years beforehand, and on multiple occasions, because God knew that humans would sin; and He knew that we would need a Savior.

Jesus Christ is God's plan to save sinners. There is just one plan. Just one. We as humans may have a plan A, plan B, etc. for any particular endeavor. But God just has one plan to save humanity. Jesus Himself says, 'I am the way, and the truth, and the life. No one comes to the Father except through me' (John 14:6). Jesus is God's plan to save fallen and frail humans.

We find this foretold event, this advent, again emphasized in Matthew, as Joseph is mulling over how to respond to his pregnant fiancée Mary.

> But as he considered these things, *behold*, an angel of the Lord appeared to him in a dream, saying, 'Joseph, son of David, do not fear to take Mary as your wife, for that which is conceived in her is from the Holy Spirit. She will bear a son, and you shall call his name Jesus, for he will save his people from their sins.' All this took place to fulfill what the Lord had spoken by the prophet: '*Behold,* the virgin

shall conceive and bear a son, and they shall call his name Immanuel' (which means, God with us)' (Matt. 1:20-23).

All this was done, Matthew emphasizes, in order to fulfill what the Lord had already spoken through His prophets. 'Watch for this, because I am going to give you a sign. It is not something that happens every day. A virgin will bear a child!'

Not only the coming of Christ, but the miraculous manner of His birth was specifically foretold so that we might take all the more notice of it when it came to pass.

The Miraculous Coming of Christ

Matthew tells us specifically to 'Behold' an angel's appearance, a virgin giving birth, wise men from afar coming to see the child who is Christ, a star that led them to Him, and most of all Immanuel—'God with us.' The coming of Jesus as the Christ is a miracle, accompanied by an army of miracles, and Matthew wants to draw our attention to how significant, how truly amazing, this event is.

A Virgin Gives Birth

It may seem as you are reading through the Bible that there is a miracle happening every few days. In the Old Testament alone there seems at times to be astonishing things happening one after another. A whole nation walks through a sea on dry ground, then is fed by bread from heaven, then is drinking water out of a rock. In another book of the Bible a man is interpreting dreams and telling the future, then some people are walking out of a fiery furnace unscathed, then another man is being cast into a lions' den but actually exits the den unharmed.

While it may seem like these miracles are constantly occurring in the Bible, the fact is the Bible is telling us about some of the most remarkable events and people and truths in history, and so it is necessarily skipping over centuries of normal days—totally normal days. The Bible skims over the stories of millions of faithful people, children of God, who served God in obscurity their whole lives without a single miracle happening to deliver them or their children from difficulty or pain. They did not watch their enemies get crushed by an angel or by a big wave in the sea. No, the vast majority of saints throughout history—Old Testament and New Testament—have lived their whole lives, faithful to God, without experiencing a single angel appearance or hearing any audible voice from heaven.

In other words, it was just as unexpected for Zachariah or for Joseph or for Mary to find an angel standing in front of them and speaking to them as it would be for any of us. It would be like an angel suddenly appearing to you on a Monday morning in your kitchen, addressing you audibly as you are about to sit down to breakfast. This is not normal for anybody. That is why we are told, '*Behold!* An angel appeared to Joseph.' This is way out of the ordinary. Joseph did not have this happen to him all the time. This was a jaw-dropping, history-shaping event. Something very special is happening here. Something supernatural is intervening in the natural world.

In Luke 1:31 an angel appears to Mary also saying, 'And *behold,* you will conceive in your womb and bear a son, and you shall call his name Jesus.' Mary was just as taken off guard, just as astonished by this event as anyone else would be. When the angel tells her she is going to have a baby, she asks the obvious question: 'How will this be, since I am a virgin?' (Luke 1:34). This just does not happen! Mary is basically asking, 'Gabriel, has someone not explained the birds and the bees to you?' To which Gabriel replies in effect, 'Why do you think I'm here? And why do you think I said, "Behold"? This is extraordinary!'

Gabriel explains further, 'The Holy Spirit will come upon you, and the power of the Most High will overshadow you; *therefore* [you're right, this doesn't happen every day, in fact only one day in all of history!] the child to be born will be called holy—the Son of God' (Luke 1:35). The Son of God! 'This is amazing,' the angel might as well be saying to Mary, 'I've been around for thousands of years, I sang out loud and I shouted for joy when I saw God creating the earth; but even I have never seen anything like this before. I have never seen anything as wonderful, as unthinkable, as God coming to earth and taking on humanity. *Behold,* Mary, this is something that the Holy Ghost Himself is going to be bringing to pass inside you.'

Wise Men Follow a Star

Matthew goes on to draw our attention to the wise men who visited Jesus after He was born: 'Now after Jesus was born in Bethlehem of Judea in the days of Herod the king, *behold,* wise men from the east came to Jerusalem' (Matt. 2:1).

It is remarkable that while the Jewish nation largely ignored the birth of Christ, these noble personages journeyed from far away just to celebrate the Messiah's birth. The Jewish people knew the Messiah would be born in Bethlehem, according to prophecy; they seem to have been quick and confident in their answer to the Magi's inquiry. Yet they did not visit the Christ themselves, nor set off as much as a single firecracker in celebration. They could see the same star in the sky that the wise men were following, but had they investigated this phenomenon? No!

When the wise men came and inquired, saying, 'We are here to see the king who is born,' not a single person piped up and said, 'I'd like to tag along with you because that's someone I would like to meet too!' Rather, the wise men continue on alone. In all the city of Jerusalem, they cannot find so much as a single person who desires to carpool or caravan to Bethlehem.

This, indeed, is worth considering: *behold,* wise men traveled months to come and see Jesus while people living next door, who shared Jesus' culture and ethnicity, could not be troubled to make room for Him in the hotel. Three Gentile Magi traveled a great distance just to come and worship Jesus, while His own people ignored His arrival. The contrast serves as a poignant reminder of how inappropriate indifference to Jesus is.

'Look at this! Think about this!' Some wise men whose names you will never know, who in fact disappear from history afterward, care enough to travel months to see Jesus; meanwhile, others do not care to see and worship Him at all. How inappropriate indifference is when Jesus is the subject of consideration! The only appropriate response to Jesus' person and work is going to great lengths, as these Gentile men did, to see and worship Him. No obstacle should stand in the way between us and Jesus.

Having inquired as to the whereabouts of the Christ-child, and being directed to Bethlehem, the wise men 'went on their way. And *behold,* the star that they had seen when it rose went before them until it came to rest over the place where the child was' (Matt. 2:9). Pastor and author David Mathis points out that 'Matthew would have us be just as shocked' with the star as with the wise men.[1] Behold, the star moved in order to hover over where this Child was. Pay attention! Take notice! This is no ordinary star. God is conducting the cosmos to bring people to worship Jesus. And God is doing that still today—still working amazing things in His world in order to bring people to Jesus.

We may not be able in every case to see the supernatural nature of God's working. It may not be a star in the sky. It may just be a person whom we happen to bump into. It may be a series of events, difficulties, losses, or pains in our life. But God is still directing the cosmos in order to bring people to worship Jesus.

Angels announce, a virgin gives birth, wise men travel for months, and a star is created and manipulated in order to bring glory to this Child. All in order to bring attention ultimately to the marvel of Immanuel—God with us. Those are the three

---

1   https://www.desiringgod.org/articles/that-crazy-star-of-bethlehem.

sweetest words you can put together in any language: 'God with us.'

IMMANUEL IS COME

We are meant to be in awe of the angel's announcement to Joseph concerning Mary's miraculous conception (Matt. 1:20), of the wise men following a new star in order to worship the Christ-child (Matt. 2:1-9), and of the divinely directed flight to and from Egypt (Matt. 2:13-19). All this is astounding! But all of this is recorded so that we will *behold,* so that we will consider the world-tilting implication of Immanuel.

This is not merely a miracle in which the natural world is interrupted or imposed upon by a supernatural or divine power. This is not, in other words, just your everyday, average miracle. Even if you put all the miracles that have ever happened all together on one side of the scale and you put this one miracle on the other side, it is weighty. This is not just God *interrupting* His natural order in order to do something. This is God *entering* His own creation in order to take on humanity, for all eternity! Jesus will now forever be the God-man. This is unspeakably glorious. Glorious, not just in doing it, but in conceiving it – not just in performing it, but in planning it.

This is an event only God could have planned or accomplished. Every human is fallen by nature, enemies of the good God who made us. God on the other hand is holy and perfect and just. Yet God loved us anyway! And so God decided that a way must be made in order for men and women—sinners—to no longer be enemies with Him, but friends! The way this happens is that the Son of God Himself came and took our place. Jesus took our place, and paid for our sins on the cross, so that we can forever be with Him.

THE GOOD NEWS IS FOR ALL PEOPLE

Some common shepherds were in a field the night that Jesus was born. To this day, no one even knows their names. Yet in his gospel account, Luke draws our attention to what happened in that field:

> And an angel of the Lord appeared to them, and the glory of the Lord shone around them, and they were filled with great fear. And the angel said to them, 'Fear not, for *behold,* I bring you good news of great joy that will be for all the people' (Luke 2:9-10).

The standard greeting when angels appear to humans is, 'Fear not.' People have been known to fall on their faces in sheer terror just at the sight of God's heavenly messengers. The shepherds here were no different. They were 'filled with great fear'—terrified! Too often you see trite little illustrations of angels in Bible storybooks, such as a chubby little Gabriel announcing the birth of Christ. In fact, the angel might better be pictured tall as a skyscraper (like in 2 Samuel 24, which describes an angel's sword extended over an entire city). The shepherds in the field, then, plainly felt puny and vulnerable and exposed in the brilliant light breaking out into the darkness, out of heaven.

Angels, we might say, are like really, really, impressive butlers. They are so dignified, so majestic themselves, that they are always intimidating when they appear. It's like knocking on the door of a great mansion; when the butler shows up, you are already intimated before you even walk into the three-story foyer. Yet their very presence, like a butler, is a reminder that there is a Lord. There is a Lord whose power and wealth and reputation puts the butler's to shame. The butler is just the servant in the house! The estate belongs to the Lord. Angels— as impressive as they are—are merely messengers. They are servants doing the bidding of the Lord of the house.

When the angels appear to the shepherds, then, their very presence is a reminder that they are announcing someone far superior in power and glory to themselves—and they buttle well, because that is exactly whom they announce: 'Fear not, for *behold*, I bring you good news of great joy that will be for all the people. For unto you is born this day in the city of David a Savior, who is Christ the Lord.'

It is amazing that an angel appeared to shepherds in a field, but the angel does not focus attention on himself or the army of angels that is about to appear with him. The angel draws attention to the goodness of the news that he brings, the majesty of the Lord whom he serves, the joyful implication of the coming of the Christ!

At first glance, this is one of the strangest scenes in the Bible. Angels appear to shepherds, in the middle of nowhere. Heavenly messengers announce the advent of the Messiah, proclaim a cosmic call to worship, and declare peace on earth—not in the halls of Caesar or the temple of the Jews, but in a grass field and to a ragtag group of socially ignored, insignificant, unnamed sheepherders. This would be like the President of the United States giving his victory speech to a handful of farmhands in a cornfield, with no cameras. Only this is infinitely more striking.

The people of God had been waiting for thousands of years for the promised Christ, who would be called the wonderful Prince of peace. But what a beautiful reality is here displayed! God in the highest is coming down to take on flesh, and so angels from heaven are heralding it to shepherds. The inexpressible condescension of the Lord is not only announced—it is illustrated.

Jesus Christ came down from heaven to save the socially ignored, the sinful, and the insignificant. He did not just publicize good will toward men: He showed good will, even to the smallest of men. The audience matched the message. The hearers represented the good news. The shepherds were themselves a living illustration of the fact that this good news encompasses all people.

No wonder, then, that the message included a call for the sinful and the lowly to give glory to God in the highest! The highest is come to the lowest; praise is only appropriate.

The Marvelous Coming of Christ

Does it seem trite to you for the Bible writers to use this word *behold* so profusely? As we have already noted, the word occurs over 200 times in the New Testament alone. And the word seems to pop up over and over again as we consider the birth of Jesus. Does it start to lose its punch after maybe the tenth time?

This is a perfect example of how words fail. They always fall miserably short in describing the majesty of who God is and of all that God is doing. This subject matter is infinitely more worthy of superlatives, of highlighting, of exclamation than so many of the small things that constantly capture our attention in the world around us—a famous movie star earning an Academy Award, or a powerful politician winning a national election, or a big weather event garnering global attention.

These things are nothing compared to *the* event of all history: God coming to be with us. God Himself—Creator of the universe, righteous Ruler over everything and everyone—gave up the perfection of heaven in order to come down to earth, take on humanity, be born in a tiny town, be laid in an animal trough for His cradle, walk among us for over thirty years, and then die an excruciating death in our place. All this so that feeble people could be friends with the holy God!

We are not meant to skim lightly over this miracle of all miracles, this mercy of all mercies, this wonder of all wonders. It is for this reason the gospel writers do what they can with the words they have while sprinkling imperatives throughout the pages of Scripture saying, 'Think about this! Listen to this! Look at this! Consider this! Be amazed by this!' They are calling us to *behold* the reality of Christ's birth and be transformed by it.

If you are a Christian, perhaps you are very familiar with the narrative of the birth of Christ. Perhaps you already know all the biblical details we have reviewed concerning the incarnation. But when did you last *behold* this marvelous event? I'm not talking about just reading it, or including it on a Christmas card, or singing songs about it. When did you last pause and truly consider this event? How long has it been since you focused by faith on the truth that God has come to us in the person and work of Jesus Christ? God's Word encourages us to stop and consider this good news. Take time to ponder the virgin-born Jesus who is God come to live with us, to be one of us.

And if you are not yet a Christian—*behold!* A virgin was once—once in all of history—with child, and gave birth to a son. They named this holy child Jesus (which means *savior*) because His mission was to save His people from their sins. He has come to be known as Immanuel, which means 'God with us.' Because He is! Jesus is God with us. Consider this one who was born with a death sentence. He died in your place, for your sins, and was raised again from the dead for you to have new life in His name. You can trust your life, now and forever, to this Jesus, who is Savior and Lord.

Behold! Linger and Consider:

- Why is it significant that Jesus' birth was prophesied hundreds of years beforehand? What does this say about the purpose for which Jesus came?

- Although the story of Jesus' incarnation is retold every Christmas season, is there anything about it that strikes you forcefully as you pause to consider it afresh?

- What do we learn about the person and work of Christ in the angels' announcement to the shepherds? Do you see yourself, and other unlikely candidates for God's grace, included in this divine message?

2 GOD'S BELOVED SON

*If we only spent more of our time in looking at Him we should
soon forget ourselves.*
—Dr. Martyn Lloyd-Jones

I once heard a pastor relate the story of a conversation he had
with a fellow passenger on a lengthy transcontinental flight.
The pastor struck up a friendly dialogue with the man sitting
next to him. 'What do you do for a living?' the man asked.
The pastor shared that he had been in the ministry for many
years, spoke of some of the specific blessings and challenges he
had experienced, and then asked the man what his profession
was. 'I'm an actor,' the man replied. Knowing that acting can
be a difficult and brutal industry to break into, the pastor
inquired, 'Have you had any success in that field?' The man
answered, 'Yes, I've had a pretty good experience so far.'

Afterward, when this fellow passenger got up from his seat,
a lady nearby leaned over to the pastor and said, 'What an
opportunity, for you to get to sit next to him!' The pastor, not

understanding the woman's excitement, asked, 'Why? Who is he?' The woman looked at him in disbelief and then simply said, 'That is Tom Cruise.'

A Remarkably Unremarkable Man

Imagine sharing personal space with one of the most famous Hollywood stars in history, and not even being aware of the significance of the encounter! Yet, the people of Jesus' day had an infinitely more momentous opportunity to rub shoulders with Immanuel Himself. The town's people watched Jesus grow up in Nazareth, and the Jewish leaders sat and visited with the young boy Jesus about religious questions in the temple. All the while, however, many of those with whom Jesus interacted had no idea that they were in the presence of the Messiah Himself!

Among those who knew Jesus—or at least knew *of* Jesus— before Jesus began His public ministry, was a man named John. John was actually a member of Jesus' own extended family. You see, a few months before Jesus' own miraculous birth there was another remarkable birth. The baby—born to faithful Zachariah and Elisabeth—has come to be known as John the Baptist.

John's parents had not been able to have any children before an angel appeared to Zachariah and told him their son was going to be the forerunner of the long-awaited Messiah.

John's life was so closely connected with this coming Messiah that he leapt for joy *in utero* when Jesus' expectant mother Mary came to visit. Those who were close to the remarkable events surrounding John's birth were known to say, 'What then is this child going to be?' because the hand of God was so clearly with him (Luke 1:66).

Zachariah, overwhelmed with the redemptive story he was being swept up into, responded to the angel's announcement concerning his son John with this exclamation:

> You, child, will be called the prophet of the Most High; for you will go before the Lord to prepare his ways, to give knowledge of salvation to his people in the forgiveness of their sins, because of the tender mercy of our God, whereby the sunrise shall visit us from on high. (Luke 1:76-78)

Despite this remarkable beginning to John's life, and despite his own remarkable ministry which followed, it appears John himself did not recognize Jesus as the Messiah until the eventful day when Jesus came to be baptized by John. Just as the prophet Isaiah had described centuries beforehand, there was nothing about Jesus' physical appearance or build that was particularly striking, or that would even lead anyone to take a second look at Him (Isa. 53:2). Jesus was a remarkably unremarkable man, in many ways.

Not Worthy to Carry His Shoes

In contrast to Jesus' unremarkable dress and demeanor, John's youth and even young adulthood were odd, to say the least. While John was a man consecrated to the Lord from before his birth and committed to the Lord throughout his life, he was first drawn apart into the desert to live there for a period of time. He was clothed in the curious apparel of a prophet, and his diet—consisting of locusts and honey—was more like a permanent fast than three square meals a day. When John finally emerged from obscurity into public ministry as an adult, his message to God's people was a call to repentance and faith. As his ministry grew in scope and influence, people came from all over to hear this strange man preach.

Yet even as his own ministry was increasing, John made it plain that he was only the forerunner, only a messenger for the greater One who was soon to come on the scene. 'Yes,' John admitted, 'I am baptizing you with water for repentance, but the Messiah who is coming after me is far greater than I am. In fact, I am not even worthy to carry his shoes! The One who is coming will not baptize you merely with water: he will baptize you with the Holy Spirit' (see Matt. 3:11).

It is worthwhile to pause here and ask—in light of John's bold introduction to the Christ—when was the last time you felt this way about Jesus?

I am not worthy to carry his shoes.

Yes, Jesus is a friend to sinners. And, yes, Jesus humbled Himself even to serve His own disciples. But this same Jesus is also the Son of God! Every particle in the universe was created through Him. It is by His strength and by the force of His will that every atom is held together. Jesus is the Word who was with God, and who was God, from the beginning. Jesus belongs in heaven, with armies of angels surrounding Him with praise day and night. Yet Jesus volunteered to come to earth, be born as a human being, and live among us.

We did not deserve this. No inhabitant of earth could ever earn such a privilege, or such a sacrifice. Essential to understanding what Jesus came to do on this earth, and how He accomplished it, is first recognizing the fact that the world was not worthy of such condescension—much less any one of us individually.

John saw this clearly, and stated it plainly: 'I am not worthy to even carry this man's sandals. I can't pretend that I even belong in his presence. The Messiah is not just greater than I am; He is everything that I am not. He is the Son of God.' Do you feel the weight of the Messiah's inherent glory, as John did? Only when we do will we begin to understand the wonderment John walked in each day, just to be the herald for the coming Christ.

Wowed By the Son of God

It is in this context that we then find Jesus coming to John in the wilderness to be baptized by him. As Matthew records in his gospel, John is so in shock that he initially even refuses Jesus' request, saying, 'I need to be baptized by you, and do you come to me?' (Matt. 3:14). When Jesus insists, however, John obliges Him. Matthew is clearly in awe himself as he recounts the events that follow:

> And when Jesus was baptized, immediately he went up from the water, and *behold,* the heavens were opened to him, and he saw the Spirit of God descending like a dove and coming to rest on him; and *behold,* a voice from heaven said, 'This is my beloved Son, with whom I am well pleased.' (Matt. 3:16-17)

If you are a student of language, you may recall that an 'interjection' is a part of speech used to interrupt normal sentence structure. An interjection is a kind of self-contained message, carrying its own meaning. This is how Matthew uses the word *behold* in his account of Jesus' baptism. It is as though he is reflecting John's own amazement as the baptism of Jesus unfolds: 'As Jesus came up out of the water—wow!—the Spirit of God descended on Him, and—wow!—a voice from heaven spoke audibly.'

John is stunned by what is happening. John can hardly believe his own eyes and ears. John is 'wowed' by the public confirmation of the Father and the Spirit as they affirm the glory of the Son. And we are meant to be wowed as well. In this chapter, then, we want to increase our own awe of the Son of God, as we consider the implications of Jesus' baptism and the events that transpired afterward.

A Voice From Heaven Speaks

After thirty years of relative obscurity, Jesus comes forward to be baptized by John. This is such a weighty event, from God's perspective, it is recorded in all four of the gospels: Matthew, Mark, Luke, and John all include a narrative of Jesus' baptism. While all of these reports are in harmony with each other, each provides us with unique insight. And as we take into account all four gospel histories, a beautiful and enlightening picture emerges. We gain a four-dimensional perspective of this momentous episode in Jesus' life.

It seems that when Jesus came to be baptized, John did not yet recognize Jesus as the Messiah whom John had been heralding. When he later gave his testimony before the Sanhedrin, which questioned him, John informed them of how he came to realize who Jesus was. John explains regarding Jesus:

> *I myself did not know him* ... I saw the Spirit descend from heaven like a dove, and it remained on him. *I myself did not know him,* but he who sent me to baptize with water said to me, 'He on whom you see the Spirit descend and remain, this is he who baptizes with the Holy Spirit.' And I have seen and have borne witness that this is the Son of God. (John 1:31-34)

John knew that he himself was the forerunner, that he had a special ministry to prepare the way for the Messiah. He knew something of the majesty of the coming Christ. Like any good Israelite, John could look at the Old Testament and see the magnificent descriptions of this Almighty God, this Prince of Peace, this Suffering Servant who would come. But it does not seem that John knew, throughout his early ministry, exactly who this Messiah would be. So while John did know of Jesus' character and holy life—after all, they were cousins—he was unable to positively identify the Messiah until he witnessed the divine confirmation of Jesus at His baptism.

We know from John the Baptist's ministry that even when Roman centurions and Jewish leaders came to him—no matter how august their position might be—John never held back from telling them exactly what God would have them to know. He rebuked the sin in their lives and commanded them to repent. John, eventually, we know, was beheaded by Herod because he would not soften his call to repentance. John would tell gruff Roman soldiers to quit complaining about their wages, and he would relentlessly point out the hypocrisy of the religious elite. As a minister sent from God, John was honest and bold in confronting sin, no matter who the person was. He was a prophet of repentance.

Yet John already knew enough about Jesus' holy life to admit to Him, 'It is not my place to baptize you; in fact, if anything, you ought to be baptizing me. If one of us needs to repent, it is me.' John felt unworthy to baptize Jesus, given the kind of life Jesus had been living for thirty years. Even at the age of twelve, Jesus had amazed the great religious teachers, the intellectuals, of His day with His knowledge and understanding of God's Word. And as Jesus grew up, we are told He increased all the more in wisdom and in favor with God and His fellow man. Anyone who observed Jesus' life could not help but be impressed by His extraordinary character and maturity. This man's life was remarkable, even though His physical appearance was not.

In other words, John felt in Jesus' presence the same way any of us would feel. We have all experienced failure. We have all seen selfishness in our own lives. When it comes to human actions and emotions and pursuits, we all know personally what sin feels like. But imagine if perfection were living next door! Imagine watching someone truly, perfectly loving God with all their heart, soul, strength, and mind—and, as a result, to observe first hand what it looks like for someone to love others more than self. This is what it meant to come in contact with Jesus, at any point during His life! What was said by Jesus' apostles about Him later was also true of those who observed

Him even in his youth: 'We have seen his glory. [He was] full of grace and truth' (John 1:14).

Even John the Baptist, who was sent to command people to repent, could not see anything to condemn in the life of his cousin Jesus. God's prophet of holiness bore witness to Jesus' blameless life, even before Jesus was disclosed as the Messiah. When the prophet of repentance comes face to face with Jesus, the prophet himself repents. Jesus is, in John's view, overqualified for the baptism of repentance!

However, after John submits to Jesus' wishes and baptizes Him, John is brought to an even greater realization, as the heavens break wide open above them. The Spirit descends like a dove and lands on Jesus; the Father speaks audibly and announces that Jesus is His perfect Son. John had lived his whole life up to this point consecrated to the Lord and knew he was heralding the coming of the Messiah. But as he baptizes this man—whom he knew in some sense as his cousin—he suddenly realizes he has not *known* Him.

Heaven itself, the residence of God, opens up above John. Just as the veil in the temple would later tear completely in two, here the heavens open up to earth in order to show there are no barriers between God the Father and His Son Jesus. And—*behold!*—a voice speaks audibly. This same voice is elsewhere described as sounding like 'the roar of many waters and like the sound of loud thunder' (Rev. 14:2). And more remarkable still are the words that are spoken.

The voice of God by itself, the Scripture tells us, makes you feel small—more fragile than a one-man fishing boat, in the ocean, in the midst of a hurricane. And three times the Scriptures tell us the Father spoke audibly during Jesus' earthly life: here during His baptism, on the mountain when Jesus is transfigured, and before His crucifixion in John 12:27-30. Each time the Father speaks audibly in order to affirm His love and His approval of His Son Jesus.

What makes God come down and talk out loud to humans on earth? A concern that we see His Son for who He is and therefore worship His Son as we ought to!

Matthew later seems at a loss for words to describe the experience of Peter, James, and John on the Mount of Transfiguration:

> And *behold,* there appeared to them Moses and Elijah, talking with him. And ... *behold,* a bright cloud overshadowed them, and a voice from the cloud said, 'This is my beloved Son, with whom I am well pleased; listen to him.' When the disciples heard this, they fell on their faces and were terrified. (Matt. 17:3-6)

Here again we see the awestruck response to the thundering of God's voice from heaven. The disciples fall on their faces in terror at the mere sound of God speaking. You may be sure, then, God had their full attention when He went on to declare, 'This is my Beloved Son! I am well pleased with him. You must listen to him.'

We find a similar response by those who hear the Father speaking directly to His Son in John 12. Jesus tells the people they must follow Him in order to be saved, and then publicly prays, 'Father, glorify your name.' In answer to Jesus' prayer, we read: 'Then a voice came from heaven: "I have glorified it, and I will glorify it again." The crowd that stood there and heard it said that it had thundered' (John 12:28-29).

Interestingly, Jesus tells the people around Him, 'This voice has come for your sake, not mine.' Why did God speak out loud? So that people could hear Him! So that people would listen to Him. So that people would know that God is pleased and glorified in the life of His Son.

Back in Matthew 3:17, during Jesus' baptism, God the Father calls Jesus 'my beloved Son.' What an intimate term to describe the affection between the perfect, unified Trinitarian Godhead! Over fifty times in the New Testament Jesus refers to God as His 'Father.' The first recorded words of Jesus are at age twelve, 'I must be in my Father's house' (Luke 2:49). The last recorded words of Jesus, in the book of Revelation, include Jesus speaking about His Father: 'The one who conquers, I will grant him to sit with me on my throne, as I also conquered and sat down with my Father on his throne' (Rev. 3:21). There is a sweet and complete unity in the affection of the Father for the Son, and of the Son for His Father.

This beautiful relationship is picked up and communicated by other scriptural writers. Paul would frequently refer to God as 'The Father of our Lord Jesus Christ,' to remind us that we cannot separate these two. Many in Paul's day, as in ours, wanted to express love and appreciation for God, while rejecting God's Son Jesus and the redemptive work He came to accomplish on the cross. Yet Paul reminds them, and us, this Father and Son are one in their labors, one in their purpose.

We should take notice of the fact that Jesus encourages us even to pray *our* Father, not apart from Himself. God is, in other words, our Father only because we are with Jesus and because He is God's beloved Son. Only when we stand with Jesus can we say, 'Our Father.' God is not our Father if we are not with Jesus, if we do not love and trust and follow Jesus (1 John 1:23).

What is the clear implication? There is no salvation apart from faith in Jesus Christ. Jesus Himself refers to this in John 15:23: 'Whoever hates me hates my Father also.' If you hate me or if you hate my message, if you reject me or if you reject my message, then you are rejecting the Father. You cannot have one without the other.

Similarly, Jesus told the hypocritical religious leaders of His day, 'If God were your Father, you would love me, for I came from God and I am here. I came not of my own accord, but he sent me ... Whoever is of God hears the words of God' (John 8:42, 47).

Of course, Jesus is referring to more than just the three times that God spoke audibly from heaven to earth. But even if we consider just those three occasions, the words God speaks concerning Jesus are clear: 'This is my beloved Son. Listen to Him. I am glorifying myself in Him.'

We can trust Jesus, the Father says. In fact we must. Jesus Himself puts it this way, in John 3:17-18:

> God did not send his Son into the world to condemn the world, but in order that the world might be saved through him. Whoever believes in him is not condemned, but whoever does not believe is condemned already, because he has not believed in the name of the only Son of God.

God sent His Son into the world—amazing! He did this, not to condemn the world but so that anyone who believes on Him may be saved. On the other hand, those who do not trust in Jesus are rejecting the Son of God. How merciful, loving, and appropriate then for the Father to speak audibly from heaven and proclaim, 'This is my beloved Son. Listen to him.'

An Angel From Heaven Ministers

Immediately after being baptized, Jesus is led by the Spirit into the desert in order to be tempted by the devil. It is important to recognize that this crucial period of temptation in the wilderness—immediately after being baptized, and just after the inauguration of His public ministry—is not an accident. It was the Father who led Jesus by His Spirit to this place and for this purpose. The Bible specifically says, 'Jesus was led up *by the Spirit* into the wilderness *to be tempted by the devil*' (Matt. 4:1). This is why Sinclair Ferguson comments, 'Jesus did not simply suffer the wilderness temptations; he attacked them and overcame them.'[1]

Jesus, we are reminded, is the last Adam. The first Adam faced Satan and fell, taking all of humanity down with him. But this last Adam stands. And so therefore anyone who is with Him will be able to stand also.

In the gospels of Mark and Luke we are told Jesus was tempted by Satan in the desert for forty days. You may have thought of this as forty days of fasting with three individual temptations at the end of it, but that is not how the gospel

---

1   Sinclair Ferguson, *Sermon on the Mount* (Edinburgh: Banner of Truth, 1987) 49.

writers describe it. Mark and Luke specifically say that Jesus was 'in the wilderness forty days, being tempted' (Mark 1:13; Luke 4:2). So for forty days Jesus is in this place not eating, and being tempted by the devil continually! And as the forty days conclude, Scripture records the final three temptations. As Jesus hungers, Satan comes to tempt Him yet again.

First, Satan urges Jesus to turn stones into bread so Jesus can feed Himself. However, Jesus replies by stating that there's something far more precious than food: 'It is written, "Man shall not live by bread alone, but by every word that comes from the mouth of God"' (Matt. 4:4). Jesus later explains His driving motivation in plain terms, 'My food is to do the will of him who sent me and to accomplish his work' (John 4:34). This is what Jesus lived for, every hour of every day! To please His Father by perfectly fulfilling His every instruction.

Satan then takes a different tack with his second temptation. He tries to convince Jesus to throw Himself down from the pinnacle of the temple in order to prove His trust in God. Yet, again, Jesus has a better idea: 'It is written, "You shall not put the Lord your God to the test"' (Matt. 4:7). Only a fool would test God's love and provision in this way.

Finally, as if to wrap it all up in a pretty package and offer everything to Jesus at once, Satan takes Jesus to a high mountain and shows Him all the kingdoms of the world, in all their spectacular glory. 'I will give you all of this, Jesus, if you will just worship me.' This is Satan's entire arsenal, pointed at Jesus and firing every barrel at once!

Before we pass lightly over this final temptation from Satan, we should probably pause and consider that we have all—every one of us—served the devil at times for far less. But with Jesus, Satan just skips over all the in-between, lesser temptations—job promotions, fame, social approval, or academic success. Satan forgoes all the little enticements for which you and I often fall. Instead, Satan packages it all together and he says, 'Jesus, you can have the whole world— all the human praise, all the money, all the power—if you will just serve me.'

What an offer! On the other hand, there is clearly a note of desperation in Satan's effort, because he literally is offering everything he's got. Yet Jesus simply replies, 'Be gone, Satan! For it is written, "You shall worship the Lord your God and him only shall you serve"' (Matt. 4:10). Jesus remains faithful to His Father through it all. This was forty times the force of Adam and Eve's temptation in the garden. Forty days of temptations like this! And yet this Adam stands. This man remains faithful.

Satan has nothing left to offer, and so he retreats in defeat. After the temptations in the wilderness fail completely to entice Jesus, we are told, 'Then the devil left him, and *behold, angels came and were ministering to him*' (Matt. 4:11).

Why are we to take special notice of angels ministering to Jesus after the temptations in the desert? Because this event puts two important truths on display. First, the humanity of Jesus. And second, the divine success of Jesus.

In the hunger and in the weariness of Jesus we see the same reality that is reflected throughout all of the gospel histories. Although Jesus is the God-man, He was not merely part man and part God. Jesus was fully human. Jesus knew what it was to grow hungry, to need sleep (even in a boat in the midst of a storm!), and to be just plain weary. In the hunger and the weariness of Jesus in the desert—angels coming and ministering to Him—we see the eternal Word of God truly has not just taken on some human attributes, not just put on a fleshy exterior in order to look human, but He has become a man.

The writer of Hebrews refers as much to this event as any in Jesus' life, when he reminds us that, in Jesus, we have a Savior who is able to sympathize with our weaknesses. Jesus was tempted in every way we are, yet without sin (Heb. 4:15). Jesus knows what it was to be truly, 100 percent human—not a sinful human, but human.

And that's the second truth we are to take notice of when we see angels come and minister to Jesus after His time in the desert. The angels ministering to Jesus are a sign, not just of His human weariness and the fact that He needs ministering, but also of the total success of Jesus' divine response to even Satan's greatest temptations. Clearly, Jesus passed through these tests with flying colors. The sinless Son of God is still sinless, still pleasing to His Father.

The angels ministering to Jesus form a total contrast to the aftermath of Adam and Eve's temptation. In the garden of Eden, rather than angels ministering to them, Adam and Eve were seeking to run away and hide from God! They had fallen into sin, and so they felt their guilt before a holy God. They were trying to cover themselves with leaves just to have something between them and the all-seeing eyes of God. That's what guilt looks like. But Jesus, in complete contrast, stands against the temptations of Satan and, *behold,* angels from heaven—as messengers and envoys of heaven—come to minister to Him. There is no breach in Jesus' fellowship with God, evidenced by heaven's angels being sent to minister to Him.

An Ambassador of Heaven Testifies

The apostle John records for us the fact that John the Baptist denied being the Christ Himself, in response to questioning from the Jewish Sanhedrin (John 1:19-28). But in the very next verse we read this as well, 'The next day he saw Jesus coming toward him, and said, "*Behold,* the Lamb of God, who takes away the sin of the world!"' (John 1:29).

What sweet words these must have been for John to speak, after talking throughout His ministry about the One who would come with the Holy Spirit and power, and be worthy and righteous and holy and fire-wielding. To finally have the Messiah in front of his own eyes, to watch Jesus walking towards him. John looks Jesus in the face and revels in the fact that the Messiah has come; and He has come to take away the sin of the world! Here, finally, is the Lamb of God.

It has been pointed out that the entire Old Testament can be summed up in the question from Isaac's lips, in Genesis 22:7, to Abraham. As they walk up the mountain together, with all the paraphernalia for a sacrifice but without any actual animal to sacrifice, Isaac asks his father, 'Where is the lamb?' That is the story of the entire Old Testament: looking for the Lamb who has not yet come. The theme of the New Testament could likewise be summarized by the words of John

the Baptist here, to his disciples, '*Behold* the Lamb of God!'
The Lamb is finally here.

Commentator Andrew Paterson beautifully encapsulates
the implications of John's exclamation:

> John the Baptist calls Jesus the 'Lamb of God'... This
> description must have meant something to his Jewish
> followers or John would never have used it so pointedly.
> They might have thought of the lamb that was sacrificed by
> Abraham so his son could go free (Gen 22). They might have
> thought of the Passover lamb—killed so Israel could be set
> free from slavery (Ex 12). They might have thought of the
> lambs sacrificed in the temple morning and evening for the
> sins of Israel. They might have thought of the lamb described
> by Isaiah in chapter 53, who was to carry the punishment of
> sinners.[2]

Whichever image came to mind, the lambs had one thing in
common—they were sacrificed to deliver people from slavery
and set them free from sin. So when John the Baptist pointed
at Jesus and said, 'Look, the Lamb of God, who takes away the
sin of the world!' there was no mistaking what he was saying.
This Jesus, who was walking towards them, was God's perfect
fulfillment of all these pictures, pointers, and prophecies
about the one who would deliver people from sin and its
consequences. This Jesus was going to be the final, perfect,
once-for-all sacrifice for sin.

John the Baptist ultimately pointed everyone he knew
to Jesus as the Son of God. And God Himself is likewise

---

2   Andrew Paterson, *Opening Up John's Gospel* (Leominster: Day One,
     2010) 17.

thundering to you today, through His Word the Bible, and saying 'Behold! Take notice of Jesus—He is my beloved Son, in whom I am well pleased.' Where Adam and Eve failed, where you and I fail, Jesus succeeded! He refused to believe Satan's lies; He refused to treasure anything or anyone more than He treasured His heavenly Father.

Behold God's beloved Son! Behold Jesus, the Lamb of God.

Behold! Linger and Consider:

- Jesus' early life was both unremarkable and extraordinary. In what ways did others find Him unremarkable? What aspect of Jesus' life does John the Baptist imply were extraordinary, even before he recognized Jesus as the Messiah?

- Satan offers Jesus one final temptation in the desert. What makes it special? Are there any ways we might be tempted in lesser, but similar, ways ourselves right now?

- What are at least two implications of the angels ministering to Jesus after His time with Satan in the desert? How should this lead us to love and worship Jesus more?

- John the Baptist identifies Jesus as 'the Lamb of God.' What is the significance of this title? If Jesus came to take away the sin of the world, could that include you?

3 THE FIELDS ARE RIPE

Missions assumes a whole new way of looking at the world.
—John Piper

A dear friend of ours—whom my kids call Uncle James—is a missionary in Vietnam. When I first met James, he was on furlough in the States, visiting his aging mother. How did he spend his time while on furlough? He bunked at a nearby homeless shelter, living among the inner-city homeless in order to share the gospel with them. In fact that's where I met James: serving him breakfast at the homeless shelter.

As we struck up a conversation over breakfast, I learned James didn't actually live at the homeless shelter: his permanent residence was a rat-infested, one-room apartment in a third-world country. Why? For the gospel's sake.

Having just returned from Vietnam myself in order to adopt two of our children, James and I immediately hit it off. As it turned out, by this time he had been sharing the gospel daily in Vietnam for several years, but without a single visible convert. I was shocked.

'How in the world do you keep going?' I asked. James replied, 'Because Jesus says the fields are ripe for harvesting. And He promises that although one person may sow, another person may reap. I may not be the person who gets to reap, but I can always be the person who sows.'

The Fields Are Ripe to Harvest

Where did Uncle James get this notion of a ripe harvest? He was quoting Jesus' words to His disciples, as recorded by the apostle John, '*Behold,* I say to you, lift up your eyes and look on the fields, that they are white for harvest' (John 4:35, NASB). This statement is made by Jesus soon after beginning His public ministry. And though it is a relatively simple assertion, it could hardly be more emphatically worded.

Before making his actual point related to the ripeness of the harvest, Jesus first embarks on a sort of quadruple prelude.

'Behold!'

'I am telling you.'

'Lift up your eyes.'

'Look!'

It is difficult to imagine more attention-grabbing phrasing. It is like flashing signs stacked on top of each other. Over half of the sentence is this 'sign' language, signaling the importance of what Jesus is about to say. Why all this preamble to making His point?

It must be that Jesus knows His disciples (and we, His readers, as well) will have trouble perceiving the reality He is describing. Jesus is making a claim that, as simple as it is, He knows we will struggle to believe. Something about our perspective, our view of the world, is about to be drastically changed.

'The fields are white for harvest.'

The context of this conversation between Jesus and His disciples is an intentional trip Jesus made with them through Samaria. As they journeyed, Jesus grew tired and took a break by a well, while His disciples went into the city to buy food. Jesus strikes up a conversation with a woman who comes to the well and, in doing so, takes the opportunity to confront private sin in her life, remind her of the promised Messiah, and inform her that He Himself is the Christ.

In case you're not aware of the history surrounding this conversation, suffice it to say the Jews and the Samaritans didn't get along well together. Actually, they despised each other. Or, more accurately, the Jews despised the Samaritans, and so—as is normally the case—when a person is despised they tend to despise back. And so that's the way it went with the Jews and the Samaritans.

Yet here Jesus is, talking to a Samaritan woman! And He's not just talking about the weather. Jesus is going out of His way to talk to an unlikely recipient of the gospel, about the gospel.

When Jesus' disciples return with food, they are dumbfounded to see Jesus chatting with this Samaritan woman. John, the narrator, lets us know they didn't say anything but wanted to ask, 'Why are you talking with her?!' After she finally leaves (after what appears to be an awkward silence on the part of the disciples), the disciples offer Jesus some of the refreshments they just purchased.

Jesus replies that He's been eating while they were away. Again, the disciples are confused. Had someone already brought Jesus groceries? No, Jesus explains, 'My food is to do the will of him who sent me and to accomplish his work.' And the very next words out of His mouth are to tell the disciples that the fields are ripe to harvest.

The harvest, then, to which Jesus refers is the accomplishing of His Father's work. This work, we see from Jesus' purposeful interaction with the Samaritan woman, is missions. It is the communication, across social and economic and cultural boundaries, of the good news that Jesus is the Christ.

So Jesus turns to His disciples, who are wrestling with all of these barriers, and says, 'Behold. I am telling you. Lift up your eyes. Look. The fields are even now ripe.' While His disciples were fiddling around with food and giving this Samaritan woman the cold shoulder, Jesus wants them to know that all along eternally significant opportunities were staring them in the face.

We can relate to the disciples' consternation, can't we? We are often so worried about putting food on the table, or avoiding eye contact with that awkward person, that we forget what God put us here on earth to do: tell others that Jesus is the Christ. Eating is just a means to that end. And other people (no matter who they are or where they come from) are not an inconvenience—they are the souls God has intentionally surrounded us with, so we can speak life-giving truth into their lives.

Behold. Lift up your eyes. Look. Jesus wants you to know the fields are ripe.

It's hard for us to see, it's hard for us to believe at times, isn't it? The fields of Christian service don't appear ready for harvesting when we feel tired and empty and barren. This is the reason we find similarly pointed encouragement throughout Scripture. Both in the Old Testament and the New Testament, the Bible is sympathetic to our discouragements. The Bible knows that we must often walk by faith and not by sight, because life doesn't always look like ready-to-harvest fields.

The psalmist encourages us, 'Those who sow in tears shall reap with shouts of joy! He who goes out weeping, bearing the seed for sowing, shall come home with shouts of joy, bringing his sheaves with him' (Ps. 126:5-6).

The apostle Paul likewise exhorts, 'Let us not grow weary of doing good, for in due season we will reap, if we do not give up' (Gal. 6:9).

The fields are not easy to work in, but they are full of reward if we're willing to patiently labor. Don't just live according to the right-now and the visible. Live for eternity, and for invisible eternal things.

So, weary and disheartened mother—trying to train your children in the way of the Lord and yet not seeing the heart-fruit you'd like to—look! Jesus is speaking to you, telling you something! Lift up your eyes! See! The field of your family is ripe for harvesting. Do not be weary in well doing; do not stop sowing gospel seed in your children's hearts, even though sometimes it will be with tears and weeping.

Likewise, if you are an overworked and exhausted father, a Christian with an unbelieving spouse, a pastor in a small congregation, an evangelistic co-worker who doesn't see any converts in the workplace, or a missionary trying to learn a new language—do not grow weary in your worthy labor.

Our encouragement, or food, must come from the fact that we are doing the will of the Lord, whether we see fruit being borne or not. In the barren desert of evangelistic discouragements, the stream that never runs dry is the approval of our Savior. On the other hand, the mirage that will never supply is the approval of other people. If you are seeking the approval of others, you may experience years—even decades—of disappointment. Your food, your refreshment, must come from doing the will of God.

Jesus tells His disciples to look beyond emotional barriers, ethnic challenges, and physical distractions to see the ripe harvest that is around them. Warren Wiersbe provides helpful insight to our struggle to believe and obey Jesus:

> No doubt the disciples had said, as they approached the city of Sychar, 'There can be no harvest here! These people despise us Jews and would have no use for our message.' But just the opposite was true: the harvest was ready and only needed faithful workers to claim it. For some reason, when it comes to witnessing for Christ, it is always the wrong time

and the wrong place! It takes faith to sow the seed, and we must do it even when the circumstances look discouraging.[1]

What about you? What things do you need to take your eyes off of, to raise your eyes above, in order to see the ripe harvest of Christian missions?

The Ripe Harvest Looks Like Sick People

Though weariness, or distraction with temporary things, are often the cause of our lackluster pursuit of missions, there is a much more significant and pervasive problem as well. It is evident in the reaction of the disciples when they see Jesus talking to a Samaritan woman. Our biggest problem, often, is not with weariness but with unwillingness. It is our inability to love and labor for people whom we do not know or do not like.

The ripe harvest, though, does not always look like we expect it to. We see this in the immediate context of the Samaritan woman's joyful response to Jesus. And Jesus seems to drive the point home even further in another interaction soon to follow. Sometimes the ripe harvest doesn't look like people with whom we want to hang out. Sometimes it looks like people we might not even notice. And sometimes it even looks like really, really sick people.

As Jesus begins His first tour through Galilee, He and His disciples are approached by a leper, Matthew tells us:

---

1   Warren Wiersbe, *The Bible Exposition Commentary*, Vol. 1 (Wheaton: Victor Books, 1996) 301.

> And *behold,* a leper came to him and knelt before him,
> saying, 'Lord, if you will, you can make me clean.' (Matt. 8:2)

Again, we encounter the command to 'Behold.' And no
wonder—there are many striking, behold-worthy things
about a leper coming to Jesus.

First, it is perhaps important for us as modern readers to
know what leprosy is and how it works. Leprosy is contagious.
It's very contagious. Leprosy can be transmitted through
inhaling the same air or touching the same object. This is,
of course, why there are so many rules in the Old Testament
about how to deal with an outbreak of leprosy among the
people. If it weren't carefully contained, it could easily spread
through the whole camp and kill everyone.

Oh, yes, and that's another point to notice: leprosy in
ancient times was fatal. Though in our day treatments have
been developed (largely due to the pioneering work of
Christian missionary and medical doctor Paul Brand), in
biblical times leprosy was a terminal illness and potentially a
pandemic.

In order to keep this dreaded and fatal disease contained,
lepers were required to dress in a noticeably different way so
they could be spotted from a distance. They were commanded
by law to live by themselves (among other lepers), and
outside the town. Additionally, lepers were required to yell
out if anyone came near them, 'Unclean, unclean!' This way
everyone could stay completely clear of them.

So it is no accident that in Luke 17 when Jesus comes across
ten lepers, they 'stood at a distance' and 'lifted up their voices'

in order to ask for His help.[2] This was the etiquette for lepers. They were supposed to stay away, avoid contact, and resign themselves to their pariah social status.

Yet Matthew is telling us about a leper who is actually approaching Jesus! *'Behold,* a leper came to him...' They were not supposed to come near anybody. Yet this leper rushes into the presence of Jesus and falls down close to Him. A parallel account in the gospels lets us know this man was 'full of leprosy.'[3] He had not just recently contracted the disease: he was in the advanced stages of it.

Yet this man comes to Jesus not only full of leprosy, but full of faith. He cries out to Jesus, 'Lord, if you will, you can make me clean.' Somehow it's hard for me to believe that the simple period in my English translation does justice to this man's words. I'm guessing this man who risked everything to intimately approach Jesus and express his faith in Jesus' healing power spoke each word with barely contained emotion.

And how does Jesus respond? We know from other accounts of Jesus' miracles that He could have healed this leper with just a word. Jesus does so on numerous occasions. But Jesus wasn't just persuaded to heal this man against His own inclination. Mark specifically tells us Jesus was 'moved with pity' for this man and his helpless plight. That's the heart of Jesus, on display for us to see. He is not grossed out by sin or sickness or failure—He is drawn toward it, because He cares and because He knows He alone is the true cure.

---

2   Luke 17:12-13.

3   Luke 5:12.

So Jesus does the unthinkable. He touches the leper! This is doubtless one reason why we are specifically instructed from the outset of this encounter to 'behold' what is about to happen. Jesus, in order to reap where the harvest is ripe, cannot do so from the safe distance of the suburbs. He doesn't confine Himself to the nice and neat people who have their lives all tidily put together. No, this physician comes for the sick. He cares for the socially ignored and rejected, the people everyone else keeps at a safe distance. And He doesn't only pity them; He touches them.

As soon as Jesus touches the man, his leprosy is healed. What a startling scene! Though the gospel writer Matthew calls our attention to this event, I doubt those who were present needed such encouragement. Their eyes must have been glued to the action taking place from beginning to end. Look! A leper running up to Jesus! Jesus reaching out and touching him! The leper, moments before white with leprosy from head to toe, is instantly and completely healed! The deformed body, probably even with missing extremities, is made whole.

Jesus insists the fields are ripe for harvesting. And then He turns around and shows us the ripe harvest consists of sick people with real and deep problems. Laboring in this harvest means interacting with people whom society may scorn. It means touching people no one else wants to have anything to do with. In other words, harvesting is not easy work. It's hard work. Just because the fields are ripe doesn't mean they harvest themselves.

Laboring for the harvest will mean getting involved in the mess and muck of people's lives so that we can meet them there with the sufficiency of God's words. There's a reason Jesus in the very next chapter of Matthew's gospel commands His disciples to pray for *laborers* in this harvest: 'The harvest is plentiful, but the laborers are few; therefore pray earnestly to the Lord of the harvest to send out laborers into his harvest' (Matt. 9:37-38).

Yes, the fields are ripe. Yes, the harvest is plentiful. But pray for laborers, because real laborers are hard to come by. This is hard, dirty work. It is often emotionally discouraging work. But it is rewarding work; it is real harvest. So Jesus tells us to lift up our eyes and see it, so we will engage in it and enjoy the fruit of it.

Jesus Has Power to Heal Our Greatest Sickness

Following the cleansing of the leprous man, Matthew records another miraculous healing in the next chapter. The setting, however, is vastly different. Instead of outside, the action takes place inside. Instead of a lone person coming to Jesus, Jesus is approached by several people. And instead of being in the presence of a leper, Jesus is surrounded by a throng of intimidating, socially-climbing Pharisees and doctors of the law—come to think of it, perhaps not that much different from leprosy after all.

Matthew relays the occasion with particular emphasis, however, not just on the miraculous *healing* by Jesus, but on the miraculous *forgiving* by Jesus.

And *behold*, some people brought to him a paralytic, lying on a bed. And when Jesus saw their faith, he said to the paralytic, 'Take heart, my son; your sins are forgiven.' And *behold,* some of the scribes said to themselves, 'This man is blaspheming.' (Matt. 9:2-3)

Why are we supposed to take special notice of this event? Yes, we are to observe yet another person coming to Jesus for help and healing. But something else is taking place as well. A sinner is being forgiven! The Pharisees do not miss the clear implication: only God can forgive sins; therefore Jesus is claiming to be God. Either that is true, or it is blasphemy. So the drama continues to unfold:

But Jesus, knowing their thoughts, said, 'Why do you think evil in your hearts? For which is easier, to say, "Your sins are forgiven," or to say, "Rise and walk"? But that you may know that the Son of Man has authority on earth to forgive sins'— he then said to the paralytic—'Rise, pick up your bed and go home.' And he rose and went home. When the crowds saw it, they were afraid, and they glorified God, who had given such authority to men. (Matt. 9:4-8)

Matthew brings us to a purposeful climax here in his narrative. He has already shown us that Jesus has power over leprosy, over paralysis, over fever, over the wind and sea in the middle of a storm, and even over demons. Jesus has power over all kinds of things that you and I don't. But here Matthew shows that Jesus has power over sin itself. Sin is the root cause of all other problems, of every form of brokenness in our lives.

Sin in this world, sin in our hearts—this is the crux of the problem. If you get rid of every other disease, if you heal every other sickness—without dealing with sin—then you are just putting Band-Aids all over a world that is hemorrhaging with sin.

The healing of the man's physical paralysis, interestingly, is a sideshow in Matthew's account. It is the 'also-happened' part of the story. But it is not the point of the story. The point of the story according to Matthew is, 'Jesus forgave a man's sins!' It was so striking the Pharisees took more notice of it than they did of the man being healed.

'Your sins are forgiven.' When Jesus spoke, He knew the cost of those words would be Calvary. He knew that in order to forgive this man's sins—no matter how good the man was or how pitiful his paralysis was—Jesus would have to die. Healing the man's paralysis would not deal with the greater issue. The man would still be separated from a perfectly good God because this man was not perfectly good.

Jesus knows in order to forgive this man's sins, Jesus is going to have to go to the cross and pay for that man's sins. But Jesus is willing. And so, He says, 'Your sins are forgiven.'

If we look closely at Matthew's recounting of this event, it is evident that Jesus read the minds and hearts of both the faithful men who brought the paralytic to Jesus and the Pharisees who questioned Jesus. Jesus looked at the men bearing the paralytic and 'saw their faith.' Likewise, Jesus interacted with the Pharisees 'knowing their thoughts.'

If you were present when this miracle took place, you might have noticed that the entire scene took place with only Jesus speaking out loud. No one else is doing any of the talking, but all the while Jesus is reading minds and hearts. He is recognizing faults in the paralytic's soul, He is reading the hearts of the men bearing the paralytic, and He is hearing the grumbling accusations in the Pharisees' minds. Jesus is aware of the whole situation.

It would have been striking to see it all in person, because Jesus, after talking to the paralytic, turns to the Pharisees who haven't spoken a word and asks them, 'Why do you think evil in your hearts?' It is interesting that Jesus describes their thoughts as evil even though their concern, put another way, is, 'Who can forgive sins but God alone?'[4]

In a way, they are concerned for the glory of God. And yet Jesus says this is evil. Why is it evil? Because they are trying to honor God without honoring Jesus as the Christ, the Son of God. And that is not possible. You can't do it! As Jesus Himself explains, the Father desires 'that all may honor the Son, just as they honor the Father. Whoever does not honor the Son does not honor the Father who sent him' (John 5:23).

To prove His own inseparable connection to the Father, as the true Son of God, Jesus asks the Pharisees whether it is easier to say, 'Be healed' or to say, 'Your sins are forgiven.' The obvious answer is that it is easier to say, 'Your sins are forgiven' because no one will know whether you stated this with authority or not. However, so that everyone present could know that He did have authority over sin, Jesus then turns to the paralytic and heals him!

---

4   Mark 2:7.

Jesus had already healed a leper by a touch, a centurion's servant at a distance, and Peter's mother-in-law by taking her hand. Jesus had stilled a raging storm with just a single rebuke. Jesus had cast out demons with just a command: 'Go!' But now Jesus forgives sins with the sheer force of divine prerogative. Jesus has the authority to forgive sins, and Matthew wants us to know He has plainly proven it.

When the crowd who was present saw all that had taken place, including the paralytic taking up his own bed and walking away, they were awestruck and glorified God. Doubtless, Matthew relates this entire episode, and introduces the account with the encouragement to 'behold' what took place, so that it will have a similar effect on us even now.

Jesus says, 'Look, lift up your eyes, see. Because I am telling you myself that the fields are ripe for harvesting, no matter how challenging or discouraging things may seem to your natural eyes right now.' The fields are white to harvest because this world is full of fatally sick people, and yet Jesus is able to heal even our greatest sickness. He is able to forgive our sins and cleanse our souls.

The harvest is ripe because Jesus is Lord.

Behold! Linger and Consider:

- What is remarkable about the way Jesus grabs His disciples' attention before telling them the harvest is ripe? Does it make you stop and consider yourself?

- There are several striking things about the leper coming to Jesus to be healed. Can you think of a few? How should Jesus' response inform our actions?

- What upsets the Pharisees about Jesus' interaction with the paralyzed man? Why does Matthew make a point of this?

- Jesus instructs His disciples to pray for harvest laborers, then He sends out His disciples to preach the gospel. Will you pray, and then become a laborer as well?

4 JESUS' TRUE FAMILY

*Our primary problem...is not that we lack self-worth, not that
we lack a sense of significance. It's that we lack awe.*
—Jen Wilkin

With my four adopted children—of Eastern European,
Asian, and African descent—it is not always easy for casual
onlookers to identify who belongs to my family. My kids often
get confronted at the Costco sample kiosk, or at any ticketed
event, with the question, 'Who is your father? Is he with you?'
And try as they may to convince the adult to give them the
food sample or admit them through the gate, the only thing
that settles the question is when I point to my children and
affirm, 'These are my kids. They are with me.'

Similarly, in the family of God there is tremendous
diversity. People of all ages, various ethnicities, and vastly
different cultures are adopted into this household. How
then can God's children be identified if not by skin tone, or
language, or political party?

Jesus was evidently concerned to settle this issue, because He actually brings the topic up Himself. The Jewish leaders were constantly questioning Jesus' own credentials. Yet Jesus was not only determined to affirm His own calling: He also made clear who belongs to Him and who does not. As we saw in the last chapter, God the Father spoke audibly from heaven in order to affirm Jesus as His Son. How awesome to realize Jesus is just as intentional in publicly claiming those who are part of His family!

So when Jesus' mother and siblings (some of whom did not yet believe in Jesus themselves)[1] seek a special audience with Him, Jesus takes the opportunity to point out His true family. Matthew records the occasion:

> While he was still speaking to the people, *behold,* his mother and his brothers stood outside, asking to speak to him. But he replied to the man who told him, 'Who is my mother, and who are my brothers?' And stretching out his hand toward his disciples, he said, '*Behold* my mother and my brothers! For whoever does the will of my Father in heaven is my brother and sister and mother.' (Matt. 12:46-50)[2]

Behold Whom?

Matthew's account here is a perfect example of how the biblical writers go out of their way to draw our attention to the remarkable events and truths they are narrating. On one

---

1   John 7:5 informs us that, during Jesus' earthly ministry, some of His own brothers did not yet believe in Him.

2   Author's translation.

hand, Matthew tells us to 'behold' the fact that Jesus' mother and siblings—His own flesh and blood, as we might say—are asking to speak with Him. On the other hand, Jesus then draws our attention in a very different direction. Gesturing with His hand toward His disciples, Jesus says, '*Behold* my mother and brothers!'

Matthew's narrative seems to purposefully set us up for a surprise, to drive a specific point home. He tells us first to look at Jesus' nuclear family, and then Jesus turns us around and says, in effect, 'No, don't look at them: look at my true family!'

Though we might be tempted, as those in Jesus' day, to be more concerned about who Jesus' physical relatives are, Jesus wants us to ponder who it is that actually belongs in Jesus' family. He literally points our attention, gesturing with His hand, to an entirely different way of thinking.

Behold, Jesus' true family! It is not made up merely of those kin to Him, or even all those who claim Him as family. Rather, Jesus insists, His household consists of '*whoever* does the will of my Father in heaven.' No matter what spot on the globe or era of the world they come from, Jesus' true family consists of His disciples who do the will of God.

On one hand, this might seem very simple: anyone who obeys God is part of God's family. On the other hand, this raises some important questions, doesn't it?

- What does it mean to obey God?
- Is every well-meaning person who is serving some god or gods doing the will of the heavenly Father?
- For that matter, is any Christian fully doing the will of God?

Surely, no matter who we are, our lives fall far short of the perfect standard of God. None of us are truly and completely doing God's will. Yet if only those who are doing the will of the Father are in the family of God, who is Jesus even describing?

Let's look together at the larger context into which Jesus speaks these very important and very helpful words. And we'll do so by zooming out until our field of vision includes two events that took place not long before Jesus makes this statement.

A Sinner Comes to Jesus

We read in Luke's narrative of a woman who encountered Jesus not long before Jesus described His true family.

> *Behold,* a woman of the city, who was a sinner, when she learned that he was reclining at table in the Pharisee's house, brought an alabaster flask of ointment ... (Luke 7:37)

Just in case by this point you are getting calloused to this attention-grabbing language in the Bible, imagine you are in the shoes of Matthew, Mark, Luke, or John. You are trying to chronicle the life, and especially public ministry, of the God-man. The eternal Word—who has existed from eternity past, and through whom God created the universe—has taken on flesh, has walked and taught on the earth, in person. His name is Jesus ... and it is your job to condense what He did and said into just a small, booklet-sized document.

It is no exaggeration to say that if every sentence began with 'Behold,' were underlined throughout, and ended with an exclamation point, it would not be overly dramatic on the part of the gospel writers.

Behold, Jesus healed life-long diseases in a moment!

Behold, Jesus commanded tidal waves as if they were His household pets!

Behold, Jesus was crucified for our sins and then rose from the dead!

What is remarkable is that *not* every sentence is underlined or punctuated with an exclamation point, that *not* every sentence begins with the command 'Behold!' Yet even after condensing Jesus' life, ministry, death, and resurrection into just a booklet-sized summary, the gospel writers choose—within that powerful, concise, hugely significant material—to accentuate certain things for us, their readers.

A Nameless Woman

Returning, then, to Luke's narrative, it should amaze us, it should scream for our attention, that Luke begins this little story with 'Behold, a woman...' There is a call to 'Take notice of this!' followed by a remarkably vague description of 'a woman.' I, Luke—the careful, technical historian who details geographic locations or political titles just to remind you how real all this history is—will not mention this woman by name.

All you need to know is that she was well known in her own community as a sinner. Oh, and you need to know that she somehow shoved her way into a private dinner just to bring her most treasured possession to Jesus, and then give Him a foot-bath with it!

We are told to take note of this unnamed woman who approaches Jesus, in someone else's house, with what is probably her life savings (it has been estimated that a stone jar full of perfume would be equal to about 20 months' wages).

Pay attention! Not to the august, socially-climbing, well-respected religious leaders who had Jesus over for dinner but to the nameless prostitute who is humiliating herself by coming in uninvited to wash Jesus' feet with her tears, her hair, and her life savings.

Her Sacrificial Gift

This is not an everyday currency this woman is bringing to Jesus. Although Luke won't tell us her name, he does specify the precious gift she brings Jesus. He does this so we can appreciate this event which was like cleaning the mud off Jesus' feet with $5,000 bills (what, you didn't know $5,000 bills existed? They do).

That's the point really: this is not an everyday currency this woman is bringing to Jesus. You didn't go to the grocery store in Jesus' day to buy bread and milk, and then pay with an alabaster box full of precious perfume! This was a commodity, a treasure, perhaps even an heirloom.

Her Forgiven Sins

Behold this woman! Her name isn't important, but what Jesus says to her and about her is. Simon, religious leader and theologian, not only doubts the woman but Jesus. He thinks to himself, 'If Jesus were a prophet, he'd know this woman is a sinner.' Jesus, reading his thoughts and proving He is a prophet, explains to Simon that Jesus does know this woman is a sinner; the problem is that Simon doesn't know that Simon is a sinner!

This woman's grief over sin and love for Jesus is evidence that her sins have been forgiven. Simon's disregard for both her and Jesus is evidence of his hardheartedness and self-righteousness.

Jesus then turns His attention directly to this sinful-but-repenting woman, and assures her that her sins have indeed been forgiven. Through her faith in Jesus she has been saved.

Our Response

Down deep, I wonder, do we sometimes think we're really not that bad a person after all? And so the response of this woman to Jesus feels a bit overly dramatic to us. It perhaps feels especially disproportionate or awkward by our current social standards.

'Ok, lady, just shake Jesus' hand and tell Him you're grateful for His help. Just invite Him over for dinner and cook Him a nice meal.'

That is what Simon is doing. And it may feel to some of us much more appropriate and normal.

But this woman recognizes she has been forgiven a lifetime of sin, not because she deserves to be forgiven, but entirely by Jesus' work on her behalf. Her expression of love is in proportion to her appreciation of the gift, and to her apprehension of what will be done for her.

Behold this woman. When you see her acting like this, does it seem out of place? Does it seem over the top? Or is it totally, understandably, appropriately joyful and grateful? The one who has been forgiven much, Jesus says, loves much.

Which person—this woman, or Simon—describes our affections, pursuits, or delights? A very religious or morally upright person can be stone cold in the presence of Jesus because they assume they're actually a pretty good person. But the one who has experienced grace, who has been forgiven much and is overflowing with love for Jesus, is ready to worship Him shamelessly and publicly.

This woman's story helps us understand what the true family of God looks like. God's children do the will of the Father by, first and foremost, running to Jesus with our sin and failure so we can find forgiveness and healing in Him alone.

A Greater Than Solomon Is Here

Immediately after the dinner in Simon's house, Jesus begins His second preaching trip through Galilee, now with the twelve disciples He has gathered. It is not long before He has another confrontation with the Pharisees, which we find related to us back in Matthew's gospel.

The Jewish leaders, who were constantly justifying their rejection of Jesus, demanded a supernatural sign from Him. Though Jesus did many miracles throughout His ministry, He never did so on demand. He is not a circus performer or medicine man. He is the Son of God.

Jesus does, however, let the Jewish leaders know that a climax is coming. His greatest miracle is just around the corner. Jesus prophesies His own resurrection! And Jesus couches His prophecy in the context of some of the greatest leaders and miracles Israel had seen:

> The men of Nineveh will rise up at the judgment with this generation and condemn it, for they repented at the preaching of Jonah, and *behold,* something greater than Jonah is here. The queen of the South will rise up at the judgment with this generation and condemn it, for she came from the ends of the earth to hear the wisdom of Solomon, and *behold,* something greater than Solomon is here. (Matt. 12:41-42)

The Pharisees wanted a sign. It's not wrong to want evidence. It's not wrong to investigate the claims of Scripture. In fact, the New Testament writers are continually inviting us to do that very thing. But it is wrong when we use this as an excuse to mount a never-ending 'investigation' that really just thinly veils our tenacious unbelief. That is what the Jewish leaders were doing. This is evident on many occasions, and none more so than when Jesus actually raised the man Lazarus from the dead, and the Pharisees conspired to kill them both in order to dispose of the evidence.

As Jesus intimates to the Jewish leaders seeking a miracle, the greatest miracle is ultimately provided in the form of His own resurrection. This is the superlative sign. The God-man coming back from the grave after being publicly and excruciatingly put to death. In fact, Jesus' resurrection is the most historically documented event in ancient history. This is why the New Testament writers over and over again invite us to investigate it—there is abundant proof to be considered.

Interestingly, however, Jesus does not merely tell the Jewish leaders that His own resurrection is a greater *sign* than Jonah miraculously surviving the fish encounter. Jesus insists that He *Himself* is greater than Jonah, who was God's own prophet. Unlike Jonah, Jesus came willingly with God's good news. And while Jonah came with a message of temporary deliverance, those who trust in Jesus will never die.

When the people of Nineveh heard Jonah's call to repentance, the entire city responded and was delivered from destruction. Yet Jesus is a far greater envoy from heaven than Jonah ever was, so Nineveh will serve as a witness against all who reject the person and work of God's own Son.

Likewise, a greater than Solomon has come. Solomon's wisdom was legendary throughout the known world, to the extent that the queen of the South traveled all the way to Israel just to listen and learn from him—an excursion some estimate to have required a six-month journey each way! Yet Jesus says, '*Behold,* something greater than Solomon is here.'

Many people imagine a Jesus who is always modest and self-effacing. Yet Jonah and Solomon were both revered, heroic figures to the Jewish people; and Jesus claims to be greater than their most effective teacher and their wisest king! And He commends the people of Nineveh and the queen of the South—both of whom were Gentiles—for recognizing the glory of God even though the Jewish leaders seem blind to it. This is one of many places in Scripture you will be made very uncomfortable if you're trying to read the Bible and think of Jesus as merely a great moral teacher.

Perhaps we don't have the same reverence for Jonah and Solomon that the Jewish people did in Jesus' day. But Jesus' claim to ultimate superiority cuts through every culture and era, and forces us all to compare our own idols or heroes to Him. Who does your culture, your worldview, revere for their powerful speaking or their intellectual prowess and accomplishments?

Are you a scientist? Then a greater than Einstein is here.

Are you a social activist? A greater than Gandhi is here.

Are you politically engaged? A greater than Churchill is here.

Jesus is in an entirely different class than the world's greatest leaders and thinkers. Even the Gentiles could see the glory of God in lesser lights. And so Jesus says in effect to His Jewish audience, 'Behold! Before you stands the Son of God. How will you respond to Him?'

Countless great leaders or humanitarians have lived throughout history. They have said a lot of impressive things and done many impressive deeds. But people don't normally talk like this. Jesus talks as if He has utter confidence in His own transcendent glory.

It is immediately following this confrontation with the Jewish leaders that Jesus will go on to describe those who make up His family. It is hard to miss the implication. Those who do the will of the Father are the same as those who are in awe of God's transcendent Son.

Behold, Jesus' Brothers and Sisters

And so, just a few verses later, we come back to where we began in Matthew 12:46-50, and Jesus' emphatic statement, 'Behold my mother and my brothers!' Who are they? 'Whoever does the will of my Father.'

From the woman who anointed Jesus with her perfume we now understand that doing the Father's will begins with recognizing we are sinners, and Jesus is the Savior in whom forgiveness is found. From Jesus' rebukes to the Jewish leaders we have learned that obedience to God also includes walking in awe of God's Son Jesus. It means repenting and submitting to Him, because a greater than Jonah is here; it means listening and learning from Him because a greater than Solomon is here.

Matthew as the narrator drew our attention at first to 'behold' Jesus' natural family. His mother and siblings—with whom He grew up in the same household—are nearby. This is perhaps to emphasize where we might expect Jesus' closest connections to be. Yet, Jesus intentionally turns our gaze away from them and instead to His disciples, to those who are following Him. These are the people with whom Jesus is most intimate, most affectionate.

These are not people of various religious persuasions. These are people who have seen Jesus as God's only Son. But these are also certainly not perfect people (even the most casual glance at the gospels reveals the fickleness and failures of Jesus' disciples). Yet they are people who have responded to Jesus' call to take up their cross daily and follow Him. Behold!

A surer sign of Jesus' love for you than being blood-related to Him is that you are His disciple.

It can hardly be doubted that those in Jesus' day took note of His purposeful family boundaries. Jesus' own brother Jude, after becoming a believer, would begin his letter in the New Testament, 'Jude, *a servant* of Jesus Christ and *brother* of James, to those who are called, beloved in God the Father and kept for Jesus Christ' (Jude 1).

Jude doesn't describe himself as the brother of Jesus, although he is. He describes himself as the servant of Jesus Christ. He would rather be known as a servant of Jesus than the blood-brother of Jesus. Why? Because Jesus Himself assures those who follow Him, those who are His servants, of His love for them and of His familial relationship with them.

And so, Jude would have his readers know, 'Yes, I am Jesus' brother. But do you know what I'm most excited about? That I'm His servant! That is what connects me to those who are loved by God the Father.'

Behold! Linger and Consider:

- We might at first think Jesus is rude to His family when they come to see Him. But what point does Jesus use this occasion to make?
- Luke tells us to 'Behold a woman...' What makes this woman's story worth noticing?
- Jesus claims to be greater than both Jonah and Solomon. In the same breath He prophesies His own resurrection. What do these statements by Jesus imply about Himself?

- Whom does your own culture hold up as heroes? How does Jesus compare?
- Jude identifies himself as the *brother* of James, but the *servant* of Jesus. What is the significance of this careful wording?

5 JESUS, CRUCIFIED AND RISEN

Do not spoil the wonder with haste!
—J.R.R. Tolkien

My family and I recently visited the world-class Cincinnati Art Museum. Every room was packed with precious antiquities, priceless paintings, or breathtaking sculpture. It seems, however, that with this abundance of worthy material the museum curators were concerned to highlight specific items they did not want their guests to miss. They lined the grand entry and exit with particular masterpieces, making them unmissable. You could not access the rest of the museum without walking through these areas. In fact, guests were encouraged to linger and look at these works especially. It's as if the curators were saying to us, 'Whatever else you see here, don't miss this!'

Similarly, there is a glut of attention-grabbing in both the beginning and toward the end of Jesus' earthly life, as the gospel writers record it. And well there might be! The incarnation—

God becoming human in order to save humans—is a singular, unprecedented event in all of history. And this Messiah, Jesus the Christ, was born in order to die. Ultimately, Jesus came not in order to teach well, or to example well, but to die well—as the perfect sacrifice in the place of sinners.

And so we will be merely scratching the surface of Scriptural emphasis placed on these subjects as we 'behold' the crucifixion of Jesus, the resurrection of Jesus, and the commission from Jesus. We don't want to spoil the wonder with haste.

The Crucifixion of Jesus

There is much confusion today surrounding the death of Jesus. Many people view Him as a martyr of social reform. Or as a well-intentioned but ill-fated humanitarian. Or even as a great religious leader and teacher. But Jesus did not come merely to reform temporary kingdoms, but to set up an everlasting kingdom. And no one was clearer on this mission than Jesus Himself.

JESUS' DEATH WAS PROPHESIED AND EXPECTED

Jesus on three separate occasions explicitly prophesied His own coming death. The final such utterance is found in Matthew's gospel, as Jesus warns His disciples:

> *Behold,* we are going up to Jerusalem; and the Son of man will be betrayed to the chief priests and scribes, and they will condemn him to death, and deliver him to the Gentiles to be mocked and scourged and crucified, and he will be raised on the third day. (Matt. 20:18-19)[1]

---

1   Author's translation.

Clearly, Jesus knew exactly what was in store for Him. Jesus' death was, in other words, not a tragic mistake, though it was a purposeful miscarriage of justice on the part of the Jewish leaders. But Jesus went to the cross willingly. Jesus was crucified because Jesus was born into the world in order to die.

In Luke's parallel account of this same prophecy, Jesus actually emphasizes the fact that His coming death is the climax, not only of Jesus' own prophecies, but of the entire arch of redemptive history in Scripture: '*Behold,* we are going up to Jerusalem, and *everything that is written* of the Son of man by the prophets *will be accomplished*' (Luke 18:31, RSV). In other words, these are not just events Jesus is foretelling; this is the unfolding of God's pre-world plan to save humanity. Jesus came to die for a purpose, to accomplish a specific task; and this moment was the fulfillment of thousands of years of prophetic anticipation.

Not long ago, I was asked to share the Christian message through the lens of the Old Testament. This is not difficult to do, because there are so many predictions and descriptions of the coming of Christ, and of His saving work, even centuries before Jesus was actually born. And nowhere is this gospel more plainly expressed than in Isaiah's prophecy—over 700 years before the incarnation! Isaiah writes, '*Behold,* my servant shall act wisely; he shall be high and lifted up, and shall be exalted' (Isa. 52:13).

Yet before this suffering 'servant,' the Christ, will experience exaltation, He will first pass through humiliation and deprivation. These sorrows are described in detail by Isaiah 53, the very next chapter. Yet, again, all this agony is not accidental. Isaiah makes this plain with at least seven references in this one chapter to the fact that Jesus suffered as our substitute.

He has borne our griefs.

He carried our sorrows.

He was pierced for our transgressions.

He was crushed for our iniquities.

Upon Him was the chastisement that brought us peace.

With His wounds we are healed.

The LORD has laid on Him the iniquity of us all.

So when Jesus tells His disciples everything concerning the Son of Man is about to be accomplished, He is not only talking about the griefs, sorrows, wounds, bruising, and scourge stripes Jesus would undergo. He is talking about our griefs being borne, our sorrows being carried, our transgressions being paid for, our sin being taken away, our healing! Jesus died on purpose, and that purpose was the salvation of sinners.

Why then were Jesus' disciples so surprised when Jesus' own prophecy came true?

JESUS' DEATH WAS COMPLETELY UNEXPECTED

As we see from Jesus' repeated forewarnings, He knew exactly why He had come and what He was going to do. Jesus also grabs His disciples' attention to alert them of His coming death: '*Behold* ... the Son of Man will be delivered.' Yet the very fact that He is repeatedly telling them of His approaching crucifixion, along with their frequent responses to this revelation, gives us an inkling of how difficult it was for even Jesus' own disciples to grasp the weighty events about to unfold.

As long as they had been with Jesus, and as much as they had heard His teaching, and as often as they had followed Him for mile after mile of miracles—the crucifixion still took all the disciples by surprise. And not just the fact of Jesus dying, or even the humiliating manner of His death—the disciples were altogether shocked by the intent behind Jesus' coming.

In both the Matthew and Mark accounts of Jesus' final prophesy of His death, His momentous announcement is immediately followed by James and John asking if they can have a place next to Jesus when He comes into His kingdom. You see, they expected Jesus to be sitting on a throne soon, rather than hanging on a cross.

Here is Jesus, for the third time, telling His disciples, '*Behold,* I will be betrayed, and crucified, and scourged,' and His closest friends reply by saying, in effect, 'Can we have more power and influence?' Clearly, they weren't 'beholding' what Jesus was saying. This would be like having someone laugh and make silly faces at you after you tell them there's been a death in your family.

There is total incongruity between what Jesus says and the reaction from His disciples. Plainly, there has been some misunderstanding. The response obviously does not match the message. No wonder Luke sums up the disciples' grasp of the situation in this way: 'But they understood none of these things' (Luke 18:34).

It was completely unexpected that Jesus would come and die in this fashion. The disciples were thinking selfishly, and so they could not understand the Selfless One. They were fixated on a power grab, and so they could not grasp the fact that Jesus had given up His throne in heaven to save helpless people on earth. I cannot help but wonder what must have run through the disciples' minds later, when they saw Jesus hanging on the cross and remembered begging for a place on His left and right hand. How their view of Jesus, and of themselves, must have been assaulted by this turn of events!

Even as Jesus' prophecy concerning 'going up to Jerusalem' begins to unfold, we are constantly reminded of how upside-down Jesus' kingdom is. He tells His disciples to borrow a donkey and rides this young colt into the city. The Creator of the universe is making His grand entry into the capital city! But He doesn't choose a spectacular chariot—or for that matter a 747 jumbo jet—but rather He chooses a donkey.

The juxtaposition of grandeur and humility, of majesty and meekness, is so great that Matthew points to it as the fulfillment of yet another Messianic prophecy, 'This took place to fulfill what was spoken by the prophet...*Behold,* your king is coming to you, humble, and mounted on a donkey, on a colt, the foal of a beast of burden'" (Matt. 21:4-5).

Behold! Your king is coming to you ... humble?! From His lowly birth, to His humiliating death, everything about Jesus is actively, intentionally opposed to the human norms of glory, honor, and success. But that is because Jesus came, not to make a name for Himself, but to remedy our normal concepts of glory, honor, and success. Jesus came to save us from, among other things, our own solutions.

Perhaps this is why the power brokers of His day hated Him so vehemently. And this is why they would stop at nothing to dismantle His ministry. Even if it meant executing a completely innocent man.

JESUS' DEATH WAS COMPLETELY UNDESERVED

As Jesus describes His own death to His disciples beforehand, anyone paying careful attention would notice not only that Jesus would die, but that He would be betrayed. '*Behold,* we are going up to Jerusalem; and the Son of man will be *betrayed...*'

Betrayed! This is amazing, isn't it? Jesus comes to save sinners, and the means of His being put to death is the betrayal of one of His closest disciples. How saturated this planet is with selfishness! There's not a square inch of earth that doesn't need redemption.

Later, Jesus Himself and Matthew as the narrator seem both to emphasize the tragic irony of the situation in the Garden of Gethsemane, as Jesus wakes His disciples after spending time alone in prayer.

> '*Behold,* the hour is at hand, and the Son of Man is betrayed into the hands of sinners. Rise, let us be going; *behold,* my betrayer is at hand.' While he was still speaking, *behold,* Judas came, one of the twelve.... (Matt. 26:45-47)[2]

Three imperatives to 'behold' in just three verses. It's as though the inspired author can hardly believe himself the injustice and injury he recounts.

---

2   Author's translation.

If you have not heard this story before, you may be filled with incredulity yourself. Why would anyone betray Jesus?! Here is the perfect friend, the most selfless and caring person who ever walked the earth. Surely if there was ever an individual whose relationships would be free of malice or bitterness or envy, it would be Jesus. But, no, even the perfect friend is betrayed by a friend.

Matthew seems to be still in shock as he recalls the event. Surely there is personal pain and grief in Jesus' heart as He speaks as well. Anyone who likewise reads the story of this innocent man Jesus is meant to be amazed that the most gentle and loving man to ever live nonetheless died an undeserved death.

Even so, however, we might respond the wrong way if we are not careful. We could be tempted to react like the Jewish leaders after Jesus told them of the parable in which a landowner's son is murdered by his own field workers. Surely, they respond, 'He will put those wretches to a miserable death' (Matt. 21:41).

That is how we would expect this story to unfold. Jesus comes, He humiliates Himself to save helpless sinners, then He is betrayed by a friend! Surely, He is done with this planet. Surely, He will destroy this miserable place and these miserable people.

That is the human response to this kind of human injustice. But Jesus doesn't respond this way. He suffers unjust, traitorous acts against Himself, because He came to save unjust and traitorous people. Jesus dies as an innocent, on behalf of the guilty.

As a further reminder of Jesus' utter blamelessness, we later hear the very one adjudicating His execution declaring His innocence! The Roman ruler Pilate, though politically pressured into delivering Jesus over to His Jewish accusers, draws attention to the fact that Jesus is plainly above reproach. Even as he condemns Jesus to death, Pilate announces to the entire mob in front of him:

> You brought me this man as one who was perverting the people; and after examining him before you, *behold,* I did not find this man guilty of any of your charges against him; neither did Herod, for he sent him back to us. *Behold,* nothing deserving death has been done by him. (Luke 23:14-15, RSV)

JESUS' DEATH WAS WHOLLY WARRANTED

Though the very ones who ordered Jesus' execution declare His innocence, we find emphatic declarations concerning the justness of Jesus' death from a perhaps unexpected source: the apostle Paul himself. Though Paul gave his life to spread the news that Jesus is God's Son and our Savior, Paul also insists that Jesus' death was warranted.

How can this be true? We have to circle back to Isaiah's proclamation that the Christ would be 'crushed for our iniquities.' Jesus was taking our place, under the just wrath of God, as He was punished on the cross. So even though Jesus Himself was innocent, when He became our substitute He was punished for our very real sins.

Paul expresses the paradox of the cross in this way: 'For our sake he made him to be sin who knew no sin...' (2 Cor. 5:21).

Jesus, committing no sin Himself, received the punishment for our sins. He took our place.

On the one hand, then, Jesus' excruciating death on the cross was wholly undeserved. The only perfect man to ever live should not have been tortured and then executed as a criminal. Yet, in this very substitution to which Paul refers—Jesus taking the place of sinners—we also must come to realize that Jesus' death was necessary.

It is absolutely crucial to understanding the Christian message for us to see that Jesus' suffering and death was warranted by our own sins!

Jesus bore the punishment for lying.

Jesus bore the punishment for thieving.

Jesus bore the punishment for rebelling against parents.

Jesus bore the punishment for adultery.

Jesus bore the punishment for drunkenness and drug addiction.

Jesus bore the punishment for proud, self-righteous hypocrisy.

Jesus bore the punishment for selfish cowardice.

Jesus died for all these things because Jesus died in our place, taking our sin on Himself and paying the price for it. God made Jesus 'for our sake...to be sin,' although Jesus knew no sin Himself!

Those then who are trusting in Jesus for their salvation are assured that, in God's eyes, they are as good and humble and selfless as Jesus Himself. This biblical doctrine is called 'substitutionary atonement.' By Jesus becoming our substitute on the cross, we have been made 'at one' with God. We have been reconciled to God.

This is the significance of what may otherwise seem like a minor miracle that immediately followed Jesus' death: 'And *behold,* the curtain of the temple was torn in two, from top to bottom' (Matt. 27:51). This huge curtain in the house of God, which had for hundreds of years separated the holy from the unholy, refusing sinners admittance into the presence of God, was torn from top to bottom (indicating a work of God) because through Jesus's cross-work we now have access! We are, as believers, as welcome in God's presence as Jesus Himself.

Yet the necessary implication is that Jesus' death was wholly warranted. If we don't see—in Jesus' scourging, beating, mocking, crucifixion, and being forsaken by God—that He must suffer because He is taking our place, then we will never see the gospel as good news. But if we come to see, as the hymnwriter P.P. Bliss, that 'in my place condemned He stood' then we will also sing with Him, 'Hallelujah! What a Savior!'

The Resurrection of Jesus

The crucifixion of Jesus, which we have just considered, is such a climactic event in the redemption story that it is recorded in all four gospels in the New Testament. And, not surprisingly, those same gospel writers take great care to chronicle the resurrection of Jesus as well. The same divine, multi-faceted, unified truth is presented from their different, yet harmonious, perspectives. And the gospel narrators are themselves clearly still in awe of the historical events they recount.

Matthew relates the discovery of the empty tomb with a barrage of exclamations and imperatives to 'behold' this singular day:

> Now after the Sabbath, toward the dawn of the first day of the week, Mary Magdalene and the other Mary went to see the tomb. And *behold,* there was a great earthquake, for an angel of the Lord descended from heaven and came and rolled back the stone and sat on it. His appearance was like lightning, and his clothing white as snow. And for fear of him the guards trembled and became like dead men. But the angel said to the women, 'Do not be afraid, for I know that you seek Jesus who was crucified. He is not here, for he has risen, as he said. Come, see the place where he lay. Then go quickly and tell his disciples that he has risen from the dead, and *behold,* he is going before you to Galilee; there you will see him. *Behold!* I have told you.' So they departed quickly from the tomb with fear and great joy, and ran to tell his disciples. And *behold,* Jesus met them and said, 'Greetings!' And they came up and took hold of his feet and worshiped him. (Matt. 28:1-9)[3]

Nowhere is Christianity more exclusive, more offensive, or more unique than at the empty tomb. And so, we are called to behold the details of it over and over again. The resurrection of Jesus is remarkable, and that is an understatement no matter how much you underline or highlight it.

THE RESURRECTION IS REMARKABLE

The resurrection is remarkable because it is historical. It is an actual event that took place in time and space. This is

---

3   ESV, though the third command to 'behold' is translated 'see.'

not a merely philosophical claim, one perspective on life among many. Christianity is based not on an ideal, but on the real person and work of a real man named Jesus. This is what separates Christianity from every other world religion, including secular humanism.

The most important historical subject of all—the historical person of Jesus of Nazareth—has been proven beyond the point of any reasonable contention. With more extant evidence for His historicity than Plato or even Alexander the Great, Jesus has left behind Him plain proofs of His own existence, even from the mouths of His detractors. As early as Flavius Josephus' and Tacitus' writings in the first century and Pliny, Tertullian, and Justin Martyr in the second century, the historical person of Jesus—and even the central events surrounding His life, death, and resurrection—have been abundantly substantiated.[4]

No event in ancient history even approaches the amount of overwhelming evidence as is available for Jesus' resurrection. If you've never investigated the historicity of the gospels themselves (by the way, that's what led to C.S. Lewis' becoming a Christian, and many others like him), I invite you to investigate. In fact, I think it is fair to say, investigating is the only responsible thing to do. This is what Matthew himself is encouraging us to do with his repeated imperative to 'behold' the resurrected Jesus, of whom Matthew himself was an eyewitness.

---

4   For one excellent review of the evidence for Jesus' resurrection, see Matt Perman's article at Desiring God: https://www.desiringgod. org/articles/historical-evidence-for-the-resurrection#fn1.

The gospel writer John speaks on behalf of all the apostles when he insists that 'the Word became flesh and dwelt among us, full of grace and truth; we ... *beheld* his glory, glory as of the only Son from the Father.'[5] The gospel writers are inviting us, their readers, to behold—to carefully consider—the people and events they themselves beheld in person, especially the resurrected Jesus.

This is because the resurrection is not only an historical event, it is an event with unmistakable and momentous ramifications. As John explains, in the context of beholding Jesus as the Son of God, 'To all who did receive him, who believed in his name, he gave the right to become children of God' (John 1:12).

THE RESURRECTION PROMISES SALVATION

John is not the only New Testament author to connect the dots between Jesus rising from the dead and the successful salvation of those for whom Jesus died. The apostle Paul likewise unpacks this connection in Romans 4:25, '[Jesus] was delivered up for our trespasses and raised for our justification.'

Jesus was not the victim of our sins, merely dying in our place: Jesus is the victor over our sins, rising again from the grave. The fact that Jesus rose from the dead displays His triumph over our sins. And so Paul goes on in Romans 8:34 to claim, 'Who is to condemn? Christ Jesus is the one who died—more than that, who was raised—who is at the right hand of God, who indeed is interceding for us.' The fact that Jesus rose from the dead and is now making intercession for us is what makes the gospel such good news.

---

5   John 1:14 (RSV).

The apostle Peter (yet another eyewitness to the resurrected Jesus) chimes in with the chorus of apostles and personal disciples of Jesus, claiming that the unavoidable implication of the empty tomb is that salvation is found in this resurrected Son of God: 'God...raised him from the dead and gave him glory, so that your faith and hope are in God' (1 Pet. 1:21).

Some time ago, as I was on hold during a business call, the operator discerned that I was a Christian and asked if she could share her testimony with me. She and her husband had been successful executives in New York City, up until the terrorist strike on September 11, 2001. That was the day she became a Christian.

She was walking down the street to her home, after having watched along with the rest of the world the burning of the towers. A UPS driver was dropping off a package near her door. She feebly greeted him and weakly expressed, 'I hope tomorrow is better than today.' But the UPS driver looked her in the eyes and replied, 'That's why we're supposed to lay our treasure up in heaven.'

The woman was awestruck on the spot. This was exactly the opposite of what she and her husband were striving to do, and yet she had just seen how literally everything they were banking on was burnable. Their whole life, with all its hopes and dreams, was combustible and temporary. It was in the consideration of that stark reality—coupled with the good news concerning Jesus the UPS driver told her about—that she became a Christian.

When we take a long and careful look, not just at the death of Christ but also at His resurrection, an appreciation for the eternal sinks deeply into our souls. God raised Jesus from the dead, as Peter informs us, *so that our faith and hope will be in God* alone. Everything else is passing, everything else is temporary, everything else is combustible; but life in Jesus will never be taken away.

It is no wonder that Jesus commissions us, then, to take this good news to others as well.

The Commission From Jesus

Remember how Matthew's resurrection account proceeded from the women witnessing the empty tomb of Jesus, to their running immediately to bring His disciples the news of it? How obviously true to human nature this is! These women encounter the greatest news imaginable—announced by an angel no less—and so they with great awe and joy rush to proclaim the good news to others. It's hard to imagine any other response.

Similarly, the resurrected Jesus sends all His disciples, in every age of the world, to do the same. Matthew relays this message in what has come to be known as the Great Commission:

> And Jesus came and said to them, 'All authority in heaven and on earth has been given to me. Go therefore and make disciples of all nations, baptizing them in the name of the Father and of the Son and of the Holy Spirit, teaching them to observe all that I have commanded you. And *behold,* I am with you always, to the end of the age.'[6]

---

6   Matthew 28:18-20.

Notice the purposeful repetition of the word 'all,' as Jesus addresses His disciples. 'I have *all* authority, so go make disciples of *all* nations, teaching them *all* the things I have taught you.'

Why?

How?

'I will be with you always.'

The force of the entire paragraph is Jesus' introductory proclamation, 'All authority is mine.' Then the promise, 'I am with you always' refers back to the rock-solid reality of Jesus' authority. These two divine proclamations bookend and undergird the more well known, but dependent, Great Commission. The great assurance and power behind Jesus' commission to His church is the all-authority and the all-presence of Jesus Himself as we engage in it. That is what gives us the strength, the power, the encouragement to go and teach all nations all things Jesus has given us in His Word.

Jesus—knowing how much suffering and how many doubts would follow His disciples as they followed His commission—makes sure they do not forget His presence with them in it: '*Behold!* I am with you always.'

The constant presence and help of the almighty, resurrected Jesus is promised to the disciples who are fulfilling His Great Commission. Therefore, we who have heard the wonderful, reliable news of Jesus' substitutionary death and glorious resurrection—who are trusting in Jesus alone for salvation—are to 'Go!' And as we go, Jesus Himself goes with us.

If we believe this, if we walk in this reality, how different our everyday life will be. Today, tomorrow, next week. When you go out into your real-world activities and leave behind the sermon on Sunday and the like-minded believers with whom you worshiped. When you are trying to remember, 'What matters?' and 'Why am I even here?', remember this, rest in this, ground your hope in this.

Jesus came for you, died on the cross in your place— bearing your sins, carrying your sorrows. Then He rose from the dead, displaying His victory over your sins; and now He promises He will go with you each day, wherever you go, as you go in His name.

Behold! Linger and Consider:

- Though Jesus spoke plainly of His coming death and resurrection, His disciples didn't understand Him. What caused them to be confused? Are there any similar obstacles to our understanding Jesus' purpose today?
- What are the implications of Jesus dying for our sins? Was His work successful?
- Why is the historical accuracy of Jesus' resurrection important? Do you believe it? If not, have you investigated the reliability of the gospel narratives?
- What does the angel tell the women to do, after he announces that Jesus is risen from the dead? What does Jesus tell us to do now?
- Are you obeying the Great Commission yourself? Give a specific example of a success or failure in this regard. How might contemplating Jesus' promised presence improve your effectiveness?

6 LIVING TO TELL THE GOOD NEWS

To fear God means that my life is structured by a sense of awe,
worship, and obedience that flows out of recognizing Him and
His glory.
—Paul David Tripp

In the previous chapter, we concluded with the Great Commission of Jesus to His church. It is a perfectly-worded commission: it tells us not only *what* we are supposed to do, but *how* we are supposed to do it. Jesus encourages His disciples in every age to ponder the power of His presence with them as they go to the nations in His name.

Now we know the purpose of our existence. How exciting! People around the world, in every age, wonder, 'Why am I here? What is the meaning of life?' Now we know, because Jesus tells us. We exist for the glory of God. We exist to spread the fame of Jesus Christ.

Why do we have the health, or mind, or marriage, or financial situation in which we find ourselves? Whatever God gives us is meant to terminate in His glory, not our own pleasure. God works in our lives to the end that the resources we steward will be used for the glory of His name! Because we really do believe Jesus died for our sins, rose from the dead, and is even now fueling the mission of His church. Whether we go to the grocery store or to Ghana, we go in His name.

We might well wonder, however, what a Great Commission life looks like. What does it look like in our lives personally? What does it look like in our church corporately? What does it look like in real world situations where our gospel witness is often received, not with ready arms but with opposition?

Sympathetic to our plight, God provides us another inspired history in addition to the Gospels, which tell us about the life and death and resurrection of Jesus. This divine account of the early church is commonly called the 'Acts of the Apostles.' It is the carefully researched and recounted story, the living-in-front-of-us-example, of how the early church sought to fulfill the Great Commission. It is written by Luke the physician, a companion of the apostles themselves. There is no better way to behold what the Great Commission life looks like.

We see it all begin in the first chapter of Acts, as the resurrected Jesus makes His final in-person appearance to His disciples....

The Gospel Is Launched

The disciples, though greatly encouraged by Jesus' resurrection, were still confused about the plan going forward. Was Jesus now finally going to set up His kingdom on earth, as they expected Him to do before His death? It had not yet dawned on them that *they* are the kingdom of Christ in this world.

Jesus meets with His disciples one last time, and He informs them that they will be His witnesses, starting in Jerusalem and then spreading to the ends of the earth. The disciples have been asking Jesus—both before His death and after His resurrection—'When are you going to do your job as Messiah and set up your kingdom?' But Jesus lets them know, 'That's your job. You are my witnesses.' And immediately after telling them this, He leaves! He ascends into heaven, disappearing behind the clouds. The disciples—clearly now utterly bewildered—stand transfixed, their eyes fixed on the place they last caught a glimpse of Jesus.

Luke, the narrator, grabs our attention by telling us what grabbed the apostles' attention next:

> And while [the disciples] were gazing into heaven as he went, *behold,* two men stood by them in white robes, and said, 'Men of Galilee, why do you stand looking into heaven? This Jesus, who was taken up from you into heaven, will come in the same way as you saw him go into heaven.' (Acts 1:10-11)

On one hand, the answer to the angels' question seems self-evident. Why are the disciples frozen in place and looking into the sky? They had just witnessed the (unannounced) ascension of Jesus! It's not every day you see the resurrected Jesus in glorified, bodily form. But then to have Him all of a sudden say goodbye and fly up into heaven?! How would we expect someone to respond as eyewitnesses to this event? The disciples' reaction seems not only understandable, but almost inevitable.

Yet the questioning of the angels drives home a specific point: why are you disciples still standing here, when Jesus just said you have work to do? You are the witnesses of Jesus to the whole world, until He comes again.

The disciples get the point. In fact, from this moment forward they grow from boys to men. The three-plus years of walking with Jesus, coupled with seeing Him die and then rise from the dead, give them the strength to face insurmountable odds in His name. Suddenly the immaturity, infighting, and shortsightedness seem to evaporate. Though they are still far from perfect, these men now have one unifying purpose. They are witnesses of the God-man Jesus.

This is the effect of knowing Jesus. Though Christians walk by faith, we walk in confidence. We know that Jesus is Lord, and that makes Him worth it all. Every lesser pursuit is submitted to the one great purpose of spreading the fame of Jesus.

UNBELIEVERS IN AMAZEMENT

As the apostles return home and prayerfully pursue the mission Jesus has given them, remarkable events begin to unfold with startling rapidity and results. The power of God is so on display that many of the exclamations of wonder come, not just from Christians themselves, but from the mouths of others who observed them.

At Pentecost, the Holy Spirit comes as Jesus' promised Helper to His church. Tongues of visible fire hover over the heads of the relatively small group of Christians. They instantly begin speaking in languages they have never before known or studied. The scene is so strikingly supernatural that Luke records the reaction even of onlookers:

> They were amazed and astonished, saying, '*Behold,* are not all these who are speaking Galileans? And how is it that we hear, each of us in his own native language? (Acts 2:7-8)[1]

This proves to be just the beginning of the gospel spreading. As the apostles 'go' in response to their Savior's commission, they preach and work miracles. Believers begin multiplying exponentially throughout Jerusalem, 'multitudes of both men and women' (Acts 5:14). This growth is, of course, not met with enthusiasm on the part of the Jewish leaders. They respond by throwing the apostles in prison. But this just presents yet another opportunity for Jesus to display His power through the early church.

An angel comes at night to the apostles in jail, ushers them miraculously out through locked prison doors, and then explicitly tells them to walk straight to the temple—the most public place in the city—and speak to the people 'all the words of this Life' (Acts 5:20). The next morning, then, when the chief priests arrive at work, they are met with the news that their prisoners are not in prison after all:

And someone came and told them, '*Behold!* The men whom you put in prison are standing in the temple and teaching the people.' (Acts 5:25)[2]

---

1   Author's translation.

2   Author's translation.

What a comical scene! It is an intentional contrast between the perceived power of men who oppose the gospel, and the actual power of the Spirit to enable the gospel. Like Pilate telling the Jewish leaders to make the grave of Jesus 'as sure as you can,' and then hearing the next day that the tomb is empty—here the Jewish leaders try to shut up the apostles, only to find the next morning the prison cell is empty and the gospel is being proclaimed in the town square. We are meant to take note of this amazing turn of events.

In response to this angelic jailbreak, the apostles are brought back in and set in front of the Jewish council. The high priest, intending to scold them, actually pays an accidental compliment:

> We strictly charged you not to teach in this name, yet—*behold!*—you have filled Jerusalem with your teaching! (Acts 5:28)[3]

Though the gospel's opponents have sought to keep the gospel under wraps, the power of God has effected the exact opposite. Jerusalem has been filled with this teaching.

From Jerusalem to the Ends of the Earth

As the church continues to grow, so do both problems and possibilities. Saul of Tarsus, the zealous Pharisee, mounts a savage persecution of the church in Jerusalem. However, the unintended consequence of this is the scattering of Christians throughout 'Judea and Samaria'—precisely where Jesus had already told His disciples they would next bear witness of

---

3   Author's translation.

Him. Philip, previously ordained as a deacon in the church, becomes an evangelist and 'proclaims the Christ' in the city of Samaria (remember how Jesus, after speaking to a Samaritan woman, told His disciples to look for the ripe harvest? Well, now they're seeing it!). Peter and John join him, and soon villages all over the region of Samaria come to know Christ.

These exciting events are followed by yet another angelic appearance, this one far less dramatic than the angel performing a prison break. This angel simply speaks to Philip in order to give him his next marching orders:

> An angel of the Lord said to Philip, 'Rise and go toward the south to the road that goes down from Jerusalem to Gaza.' This is a desert road. And he rose and went. And *behold,* an Ethiopian, a eunuch, a minister of the Candace, queen of the Ethiopians, in charge of all her treasure, had come to Jerusalem to worship and was returning; seated in his chariot, he was reading the prophet Isaiah. (Acts 8:26-28, RSV)

What are the chances? An angel tells Philip to travel to a certain place. When Philip arrives—would you look at that—he finds a man reading a prophecy concerning the Messiah and wondering, 'Who is this talking about?' And so Philip is able to tell him about Jesus, baptize him on the spot, and send him on to Africa with the good news!

In the very next chapter, Saul the ultra-religious Pharisee has become the chief adversary of the Christian church and is going to great lengths to snuff out this movement. He imprisons and tortures Christian believers, compelling them to blaspheme. But as Saul travels to Damascus to continue his campaign of terror, Jesus Himself appears to him, changes his heart, and calls him to be a witness for Christ. With Jesus, wonders truly never cease.

Jesus sends Saul-soon-to-be-Paul to a Christian in Damascus named Ananias, and then appears to Ananias telling him to help Saul.

> And the Lord said to him, 'Rise and go to the street called Straight, and at the house of Judas look for a man of Tarsus named Saul, for *behold,* he is praying... (Acts 9:11)

This religious zealot Saul, as a Pharisee, had prayed thousands of prayers without ever praying. *Behold,* he is only now truly praying for the first time in his life. Because now he is coming to God through Jesus Christ. Everything else is just empty religion.

In the following chapters, Acts 10 and 11, we encounter a pivotal point in the early church in which the gospel spreads now to the Gentiles. A godly Roman centurion by the name of Cornelius had been prayerfully pursuing God for help and direction. God answers by directing Cornelius to send men to ask the apostle Peter for help.

The problem is, Peter—although a good Christian—is also still a good Jew. He considers any Gentile (non-Jew) to be filthy and unclean. They are not even to be touched. Maybe he had stretched himself to interact with Samaritans, but that was as far as he was willing to go.

Until Jesus appears to Peter in a vision. Peter sees a great sheet, filled with non-kosher, unclean food. Jesus commands

Peter to eat, but he refuses. Jesus rebukes Peter, telling him not to consider anything unclean that God has made clean. For good measure, the lesson is repeated three times.

It may be easy for many of us today to look down on Peter. 'What in the world, Peter? Why would you need God to teach you this lesson, that you are not better than other people or that other people are not unclean?' But consider this: what if God told you to eat garbage? If Jesus appeared to you in a similar vision to Peter's and said, 'I know garbage smells bad. I know it tastes bad. But I have worked an amazing miracle and now garbage is going to be good for you. So, go eat garbage!'

Would you struggle with such a command? Wouldn't you maybe wrestle at least a little? Wouldn't you wonder if perhaps there weren't something else just as good for you, but that wouldn't smell and taste bad? This is what it was like for Peter, who for his whole life had lived clean and now is told to go and rummage in the garbage bin. Peter couldn't imagine how it could be God's will for him to touch filthy things.

What could this vision possibly mean? Peter doesn't have to wait long to find out, because again God is plainly on the move:

> Now while Peter was inwardly perplexed as to what the vision that he had seen might mean, *behold,* the men who were sent by Cornelius, having made inquiry for Simon's house, stood at the gate... (Acts 10:17)

This is no accident. God is working on both sides to bring the gospel to the Gentiles and the Gentiles to Himself. When Peter goes with the men to Cornelius' house, he shares the good news concerning Jesus. Cornelius and his entire household embrace the gospel, and the New Testament church discovers that 'to the Gentiles also God has granted repentance that leads to life' (Acts 11:18).

Who knows what amazing doors might open for us as well, if we start going out of our way—and out of our comfort zones—to proclaim who Jesus is and what He has done?

Now at this point, however, we might all be willing to sign up to be Jesus' witnesses to the ends of the earth! Angels appearing to us, miracles preparing the way for us, visions followed by immediate and ready-made conversions—sign me up for the next mission trip! Oh, sure, we may have to spend a night in jail but, hey, that's nothing my guardian angel can't handle.

But these are not the only stories in the book of Acts. Intertwined in the very narratives we have just considered are also moments of great suffering and loss. The apostles were beaten and told to stop preaching. Stephen was stoned to death for calling people to repentance and faith in Christ. And Saul of Tarsus harmed countless Christians before he became one himself.

Soon after the Gentiles receive the gospel, in Acts 12 James becomes the first apostle to be martyred. In fact, history tells us eleven of the twelve remaining apostles would eventually follow him as Christian martyrs, including the apostle Paul.

We are reminded that, not only is life given to us for us to tell the good news concerning Jesus Christ, but it may actually cost us our lives! And so Paul's own testimony in Acts 20 is a timely one ....

A Faithful Testimony Is Better Than Life

After the apostle Paul is converted on the road to Damascus, Jesus calls him to be a minister to the Gentiles. After many travels, planting many churches throughout the Gentile world, Paul concludes his third missionary journey by returning to Jerusalem. But Paul first calls together a group of leaders from the church in Ephesus, and informs them his going to Jerusalem will, as prophesied, result in his imprisonment. His parting words to these Ephesian elders are striking to them, and should be to us as well.

> And now, *behold,* I am going to Jerusalem, constrained by the Spirit, not knowing what will happen to me there, except that the Holy Spirit testifies to me in every city that imprisonment and afflictions await me. But I do not account my life of any value nor as precious to myself, if only I may finish my course and the ministry that I received from the Lord Jesus, to testify to the gospel of the grace of God. And now, *behold,* I know that none of you among whom I have gone about proclaiming the kingdom will see my face again. (Acts 20:22-25)

Although there are numerous things to consider in Paul's passionate address, let's consider three specific lessons we should not miss:

1) AFFLICTION AWAITS THOSE WHO FAITHFULLY TESTIFY TO THE GOSPEL.

Paul admits there is much he does not know about what will to happen to him in the future. Paul goes to Jerusalem 'not knowing' exactly what that will involve, what tomorrow will hold. Yet he does know one thing for certain: he knows imprisonment and affliction await him. Paul goes on to say he knows he will not see the Ephesian elders—dear friends—again (verse 25), and that he also knows after he leaves the church at Ephesus he will be attacked by false teachers (verse 29). In other words, Paul knows just enough to terrify any reasonable person!

Clearly, following where the Spirit leads—as Paul is doing here—may mean being content not to know tomorrow in detail. For those of us who are compulsive planners, this is all the affliction needed to make us reconsider Christian service!

Will my family be safe if we move to the inner city to minister?

How will my family react if I tell them I'm considering becoming a Christian (I mean a real one, who lives every day for Jesus)?

What if we get sick in a third-world country?

What if we make a big stand for Jesus that costs us dearly, and then don't see any fruit from our effort?

What will it mean for my grade if I tell the professor I disagree with what she said in class about the Bible?

What if...?

On the one hand, we are not told and so will not know what to expect when we live publicly and shamelessly for the fame of Jesus. Our lives may be full of uncertainty; our course will not always be chartable. On the other hand, like Paul, the one thing we can be sure of is that following Jesus will cost us dearly. It will mean taking up our cross daily. Paul does not walk on a path of roses as he goes to Jerusalem to share the gospel.

Doctor David Livingston moved to Africa in the 1800s with his family because 'the smoke of a thousand villages' was burning in his heart. He thought of all the people in Africa who had never heard of Christ. But the day they got off the boat his wife became ill and then died. Don't you think he wondered to himself, 'I need to get back on that boat and get back to England. What am I doing here?!'

Affliction awaits those who testify to the gospel. But that is not all that awaits them. Yes, there are a lot of 'what ifs' when you sign on to the Great Commission life, but there are also a lot of promises. Which leads us to our second lesson from Paul.

2) ALTHOUGH THE COST OF LIVING FOR THE GOSPEL IS HIGH, IT IS NOTHING.

Yes, following Jesus without reserve will mean giving up personal comfort, personal schedules, personal popularity, and personal ambitions. But what we get in return is the person of Jesus. Paul's great concern is following after his Lord Jesus. The fulfillment of Jesus' mission is Paul's great reward for everything he suffers.

In fact, for Paul the cost doesn't even compare to the joy. My life is not the valuable thing here, Jesus is! The reward for faithfulness, of spreading the fame of Jesus, is greater than the pain of every loss it may cost.

This means the joy of obeying Jesus and staying with your unbelieving spouse is greater than the daily pain of enduring his or her criticisms; the joy of sacrificially giving to world missions is greater than the loss it means to your banking account; the joy of patiently waiting on God's timing and direction is greater than the immediate pleasure of just doing whatever gets you out of your current trial.

3) Living to testify to the gospel may not only mean pain because of its enemies, but pain because you have to leave friends.

Some people, it is true, are called to Timothy-like Great Commission work, staying in one place for a long time and faithfully discipling in one church or area. But others are called to Paul-like Great Commission work, going to new places and leaving old comfort zones in order to pursue the fame of Jesus to the ends of the earth.

For me and my family, it initially meant moving eight hours away from where I grew up. That was one of the hardest years of my life. And then sixteen years later, it meant us moving to another country. That was *the* hardest year of my life. No comfort zone is safe when we follow a crucified Savior. But even if we have to go far from familiar territory, we will not be the first.

Behold the weightiness of Paul's mission statement. It is impossible to seriously ponder his words and remain unaffected by their import. Following hard after Jesus— obeying His Word and being His witnesses to the ends of the world—will cost us everything, but it is abundantly worth it. The joy of Jesus is greater than the pain of whatever it costs you to follow Him.

If you have never followed Jesus before, can you see the upside-down wisdom of Jesus' kingdom? That to follow the Creator of the world leads to certain joy, whereas to make a god out of this world leads to certain disappointment?

Behold! Not just the sorrow of Christians in the book of Acts being persecuted for their faith, but the resounding, everlasting joy that echoes from their purposeful and single-minded pursuit of Jesus Christ. The joy of following Jesus is the one thing in all the world that is worth living for every day of your life, in every season of your life, no matter what it may cost you.

Behold! Linger and Consider:

- What are some of the behold-worthy events in the book of Acts? Do any in particular strike you as instructional or encouraging?
- What were some of the ways even unbelievers were impressed with the spread of the gospel in Jerusalem?
- Why is Peter's going to Cornelius' home such a remarkable event? What might be a similar struggle for Christians today?
- What did Paul know or not know, as he anticipated traveling to Jerusalem to conclude his third journey? Are there similar certainties or uncertainties to which you as a Christian are called today?

7 A FOUNDATION OR A STUMBLING STONE?

God's love is the most awesome thing about Him.
—Sinclair Ferguson

Everybody loves Love. The virtues of love have been extolled from time immemorial, and love is still recognized today by people the world over as one of the last objectively virtuous virtues. Plato, some 300 years before Christ, paid this tribute to love: 'Love is the joy of the good, the wonder of the wise, the amazement of the gods.'

In Love With Love

Love was the theme of bards in the Middle Ages, was embraced by the Romantics of the eighteenth century, and is still extolled by countless cultures today. Love is the subject of urban graffiti, the slogan of smooth-talking politicians, and the theme of copious lyricists.

'Love is the key...' contends one songwriter. Another famously observes, 'Love is a many-splendored thing.' But perhaps the most well-known contemporary homage to love was contributed by John Lennon in 1967. At the height of the Vietnam War, the BBC commissioned The Beatles to write a song for *Our World*, the first ever live, international satellite television production. The BBC requested that the song contain a simple message that would be understood by viewers of all nationalities: *All You Need Is Love* was the result.

When the broadcast aired on live television, The Beatles were joined on stage by The Rolling Stones, among others, for this special occasion. The message of the song was true to its prescription, if a little redundant:

> Love, love, love, love, love, love, love, love, love.
> All you need is love, all you need is love,
> All you need is love, love, love is all you need.

When we consider the timeless attraction of Love to the masses, however, we are made to ponder exactly what is meant when the Bible insists 'God is love.' Is Scripture merely jumping on the bandwagon of love, or is it saying something entirely counter-cultural, no matter what the current culture may be?

Paul makes a startling claim in his letter to the Christians in Rome. He pictures Jesus Christ as the pivot-point of all of history, and all of humanity. How we relate to Christ determines how we relate to God. God is love, we learn, but love is not God. Love cannot take the place of Christ and still be pleasing to God. Paul writes in Romans 9:33:

> As it is written, '*Behold,* I am laying in Zion a stone of stumbling, and a rock of offense; and whoever believes in him will not be put to shame.'

Behold, Jesus Christ is the great cornerstone of history. And either we are building our life on Him, or we are stumbling over Him by taking offense at Him. According to Paul (and other writers, as we will see, in both the Old and New Testaments), love is not the key to life: Jesus is. Love is not all we need, Jesus is. God's love, we learn, is the most awesome thing about Him; and it is has everything to do with Jesus.

God Is the One Laying This Stone

Notice in Romans 9:33 that Paul begins his claim about Jesus with, 'As it is written...' This idea of the Messiah being the great cornerstone of history did not originate with Paul. Paul is actually quoting the prophet Isaiah, who lived over 700 years before Paul. God has been speaking of the Messiah in this way for centuries. God is the one laying this stone. And though the Messiah is a 'stone of stumbling' to some, God sends the Messiah out of mercy.

> Because you have said, 'We have made a covenant with death ... for we have made lies our refuge, and in falsehood we have taken shelter'; therefore thus says the Lord God, '*Behold,* I am the one who has laid as a foundation in Zion, a stone, a tested stone, a precious cornerstone, of a sure foundation ...' (Isa. 28:15-16)

It is God's mercy that leads Him to lay this foundation stone. God looks at people who are ultimately in love with death, because they are putting their hope in illusions; they are making lies their refuge. Rather than running to God, they are trusting in every empty thing imaginable as their shelter.

God sees people who are running away from Him, and He chases after them! He proclaims to them a sure foundation instead of the quicksand of their own solutions. Those who build their lives on this foundation will live forever instead of perishing for certain. Or as Paul puts it later when he quotes Isaiah, they 'will never be put to shame.'

Whether it is Isaiah prophesying of the Messiah to come, or Paul looking back at Jesus as the Christ, we are meant to see that Jesus is either your sanctuary, your refuge, your foundation—on whom eternal life is built—or else Jesus is a stone of stumbling, over whom you trip on your self-destructive way to eternal death.

Jesus is God's watershed revelation to the world. God's own righteous character, and God's only way of salvation for self-destructive sinners, are wrapped up and perfectly reflected in the person and work of Jesus Christ. Whether you and I recognize and honor and believe in Jesus or not, God has set Him as the immovable foundation stone of salvation or of judgment.

The psalmist would write of this Messiah, 'The stone that the builders rejected has become the cornerstone. This is the LORD's doing; it is marvelous in our eyes' (Ps. 118:22-23). This is the Lord's doing. Jesus is the Savior God Himself has sent. God is the one who has laid this foundation stone.

To Some Jesus Is a Stone of Stumbling

One might think that when God Himself sends the solution for humanity's total salvation, in the perfect person of Jesus no less, all the world would celebrate and receive Him with open arms. But, no, the covenant we have made with death is a strong one, entered into willingly, because we would rather die eternally than rely on God forever. When people come face-to-face with perfection Himself, they react in one of two ways: they are either irresistibly attracted to Jesus and put their faith in Him, or they are repelled by the unrelenting glory of God they see in Him.

What makes the difference? What makes one woman fall down, break open her life's savings, and pour it on Jesus feet out of gratitude, while one of His closest disciples is betraying Him to make a little extra money? Sure, on a surface level, we might guess that the woman feels helped by Jesus and the disciple feels somehow disappointed by Jesus. But surface explanations don't suffice. There are too many contrasts, too many people either hailing Jesus as their greatest hope, or treating Him like their greatest threat.

The apostle Peter gives us a deeper look at what is going on. Interestingly, Peter quotes from the same passage in Isaiah that Paul alluded to as well. And Peter makes the sure-to-surprise claim that people are responding differently to Jesus—in every age—because they are beforehand set apart for salvation or not. Peter explains that those who believe on Jesus do so because they are among those 'chosen' people through whom God has purposed to bring joyful praise to Himself; while those who stumble at the word do so because they are dead set on disobeying God's Word, 'destined' to stumble then at Jesus.

> For it stands in Scripture: '*Behold,* I am laying in Zion a stone, a cornerstone chosen and precious, and whoever believes in him will not be put to shame.' So the honor is for you who believe, but for those who do not believe, 'The stone that the builders rejected has become the cornerstone,' and 'A stone of stumbling, and a rock of offense.' They stumble because they disobey the word, as they were destined to do. But you are a chosen race, a royal priesthood, a holy nation, a people for his own possession, that you may proclaim the excellencies of him who called you out of darkness into his marvelous light. (1 Pet. 2:6-9)

Peter is here describing the widely varying responses to Jesus and, while placing the responsibility for unbelief squarely on the shoulders of those who reject Jesus, Peter plainly insists that those who 'honor' Jesus do so—not because of some innate wisdom or superior insight on their part,—but because they are set apart by God. Faith in Jesus, it turns out, is the sovereign and uninfluenced work of God in the hearts of His people.

Before we unpack this teaching further, we should probably mention that Paul is making the identical point back in Romans. Before quoting Isaiah in Romans 9:33, Paul provides examples from biblical history of people who either responded to God in obedience or in rebellion. Paul brings up the twin brothers Jacob and Esau who are brought up by the same parents, even born at the same time. Yet their destinies could not be more disparate. Paul speaks of Pharaoh, who steadfastly rejects God's Word even as Moses is God's meek servant—though they are both brought up in the royal household. What makes the difference? Paul concludes it must not depend on birth, or rank, or any other human factor: 'it depends not on human will or exertion, but on God, who has mercy' (Rom. 9:16). The difference-maker is God's mercy. Those who stumble over Jesus do so because of their own poor choices, yet those who build on Jesus as the foundation of their lives do so—not because of their own goodness—but because of God's mercy to intervene in their hearts and lives.

God's mercy is not according to national affiliation or according to blood relation. God's election is not based on human efforts or connections, but according to His own purpose to have mercy. Or, to use Peter's language, it is by God's choice. And yet it is also by our choice in a sense as well. Because all of this says something about the depth of our own heart's self-deception.

Why would anyone reject perfection when they saw it in the person of Jesus Himself? Why would any of us make a covenant with death in the first place, choosing to walk away from God rather than follow His healthful and holy ways? There is a preexisting condition, a deadness of heart—our sinful nature—that predisposes us toward self-destruction rather than toward God's freely-offered salvation. The fact is, as Paul and Peter both plainly unpack in their letters, death is the result of our own plan while mercy is the result of God's.

This is why the psalmist would describe damnation in the shocking terms of God actually allowing people to get their own way: 'I gave them over to their stubborn hearts, to follow their own counsels' (Ps. 81:12). Sin results in separation from God. But here we are also reminded that it means being joined completely to our own desires and schemes. At first glance, this might not sound so bad. The thought of being married to our own desires and plans doesn't seem to be much of a penalty. In fact, isn't that more like what we call a dream come true? But in reality this is judgment; this is punishment. Those who persist in sin and rebellion God leaves to their own stubborn pursuits and allows them to walk in their own counsels.

The person who is left to her own counsel finds that she is like a blind person at the street corner, without a guide. She is free to walk any direction she pleases, but there is danger and destruction on every side. As C.S. Lewis explains, there are two kinds of people in the end: those who say to the Father, 'Thy will be done,' or those to whom the Father says, 'Thy will be done.' The great punishment for sin is getting our own way.

The fact, then, that God does not have mercy on everyone is not what should surprise us most. It is the fact that God has mercy on anyone. Mercy is not a birthright: it is an undeserved benevolence. It is God intervening in our own self-destructive, hell-bent path and turning our hearts back to Himself.

Whoever Believes in Jesus Will Not Be Put to Shame

What is your response to Jesus? Just stop for a moment and ponder. Because this is the question that Paul's statement— if we really 'behold' it at all—presses us to consider. There are only two kinds of people in the world: either those who stumble at the idea of God's perfect Savior Jesus, or those who trust in Him and will therefore never ultimately be put to shame. What is *your* response to Jesus? Do you stumble over Him as an obstacle to the way you want to do things, or are you building your whole life on Jesus as your cornerstone? Clearly, it is my desire as I write this book that you will be among those who, by God's mercy, believe in Jesus. And this was Paul's desire as well for those around him.

It is noteworthy that in the context of Romans 9—where we find some of the New Testament's strongest teaching on the sovereignty of God in salvation—Paul in this very context expresses his passion to see others saved. The language with which he opens the chapter could hardly be stronger:

> I am speaking the truth in Christ—I am not lying; my conscience bears me witness in the Holy Spirit—that I have great sorrow and unceasing anguish in my heart. For I could wish that I myself were accursed and cut off from Christ for the sake of my brothers, my kinsmen according to the flesh. (Rom. 9:1-3)

It is difficult to imagine a more emphatic lead-in than Paul's here: 'I am speaking the truth! No, really, I am not lying. My conscience is clear before God.' Paul wants us to know that what follows is not a flighty passion or a flippant exaggeration.

And what is it Paul is taking such great pains to communicate? 'I am grieving with constant anguish in my heart.' About what? 'I long to see my own kin (the Jewish people) come to know Christ. In fact, I would take their curse myself—cut off from Christ—if I could see them be saved.'

Paul has just shared one of the most glorious promises of eternal security in all of Scripture: nothing in all creation 'will be able to separate us from the love of God in Christ Jesus our Lord' (Rom. 8:39). Then in the very next breath Paul expresses his great sorrow that his own people do not have this secure salvation. He actually expresses he would be willing to be damned himself if it would mean the salvation of his kindred. This is such a strong statement we dare not carelessly take it on our lips! Paul certainly doesn't. And it is so powerful we could probably spend the rest of this book just considering that one statement further. What is perhaps just as arresting, however, is that this is not the only such strong statement in the Bible. Moses had expressed the same intense love and interest for his people in his day. After pleading with God to forgive their sin, Moses offered to take their place if need be: 'But now, if you will forgive their sin—but if not, please blot me out of your book that you have written' (Exod. 32:32).

Clearly, for both Paul and Moses, embracing God's sovereignty in salvation fed, rather than hindered, their desires for the salvation of those around them. It did not lead them to fatalism but to fervency.

In this, they are following the footsteps of Jesus Himself. Jesus would declare His gratitude that His Father, the Lord of heaven, had hidden truth from the wise of this world while revealing it to the childlike. Then Jesus would die for them both. Jesus both reveled in His Father's sovereign judgment, and longed to see people saved.

It is because of his Christ-like heart that Paul speaks, then, in Romans 9:33 of Jesus as the stumbling stone for many people, and then in the very next verse expresses his prayer for these people: 'Brothers, my heart's desire and prayer to God for them is that they may be saved' (Rom. 10:1).

How should we apply Paul's balance in our own Christian walk? If we want to have Paul's eternal perspective in daily life, we must embrace the full spectrum of Paul's theology. The preacher of sovereign grace also pleads for God to save sinners! Indeed, surely it was *because* Paul believed *in* God's sovereign power to save sinners that Paul was passionately engaged in prayer *to* God for the salvation of others. What greater motivation to prayer could there be than knowing that God actually has the power and authority to answer those prayers?

It brings great joy and freedom as we—like Paul—yearn deeply and pray constantly for the salvation of others. What good would it be to pray for my children's health or grades if I could not pray for the one thing in all the universe that I know matters most—the salvation of their souls? What a sorrow it would be if I could not talk to God about the souls of my loved ones, when God Himself tells me in His Word that the eternal things are the important things.

Yet, even as I pray for the princes of the world and my princess in her bunk bed, I must pray—as always—'not my will, but Yours, be done.' As with every other prayer, I must be willing to trust the goodness and wisdom of God to do what is right and best. He is, after all, the God of goodness and mercy. I bring my greatest requests, my heart's deepest desires, and I lay them at His feet. And in Jesus' name, I trust that God will hear and do according to His good pleasure.

Behold! Linger and Consider:

- Everyone seems to be in love with the idea of 'love.' But what is different about God's love? Why doesn't everyone love the way God shows love?

- Paul insists that God is the one who has placed Jesus as the great cornerstone of history. Why does Paul say it was needed for God to send Jesus? What was our situation by nature?

- What, according to Paul, makes the difference between those who are offended by Jesus, and those who trust in Him?

- What is the result of Paul's belief in the sovereignty of God over salvation? If God chooses to have mercy on some, and not on others, should that change the way we feel and pray?

8 NOW IS THE DAY OF SALVATION

To become a Christian is to become alive to beauty.
—Dane Ortlund

Eternal life includes today. It is not merely a future event or a far away hope. The person who is trusting in Jesus is even now experiencing the supernatural blessings of the cross. The person who comes to faith in Christ departs the road that leads to death and embarks on the journey of everlasting life. Eternal life is therefore not only crucial because you or I might die today; it is vital because you and I are alive today. Every moment has eternal significance.

Every act, every decision, every thought in which we engage as Christians is a product of God's saving work in our lives. Just as every part of our nature has been tainted with sin as fallen humans, every part of our new life in Christ is influenced by His Spirit's work in and through us. We, right now, have Jesus living inside us as believers in Christ!

This is why John Piper writes, 'Being a Christian means experiencing the supernatural every day. Living as new creatures in Christ is amazing beyond calculation ... It may seem strange, but we have to be taught that we are walking miracles.'[1] And this is why Paul writes, in his second letter to the Christians in Corinth:

> *Behold,* now is the favorable time; *behold,* now is the day of salvation. (2 Cor. 6:2)

We spent the first several chapters of this book 'beholding' the extraordinary claims and supernatural events recorded in the testimony of the Gospels, and then the remarkable zeal and unflinching testimony of the apostles and early Christians in the book of Acts—all this couched in the form of historical narrative. But the Bible doesn't just call our attention to amazing events in history; it also provides us explicit Christian teaching concerning those events and their significance, their implication for us.

For this reason the letters of Paul or John or Peter are just as important to focus our attention on as the first-hand historical accounts of Jesus' life and death and resurrection. And this is why Paul purposefully grabs the attention of his readers in 2 Corinthians and specifically tells us twice in the same breath to 'behold' the salvation that is in Jesus. This passage, and the context surrounding it, is one of the premier texts in Scripture regarding the 'newness' of the New Testament that is in Christ.

---

1   https://www.desiringgod.org/articles/the-incalculable-wonder-of-being-a-christian.

Everything is New For Those in Christ

Backing up from Paul's statement 'now is the day of salvation,' in the chapter immediately preceding, Paul calls our attention to a foundational reality for every Christian: 'If anyone is in Christ, he is a new creation. The old has passed away; *behold, the new has come*' (2 Cor. 5:17). Christ's entry into the world and into an individual's soul makes everything different, makes everything new.

IN THE BIG PICTURE: THE OLD COVENANT IS PASSED AWAY

Jesus coming into the world was not just a significant historical event in a line of historical, significant events. It's not as if the study of history should include Pharaoh and the Egyptian dynasties, Caesar and the Roman Empire, and then don't forget to fit in Jesus and Christianity. No! Paul says everything is brand new in Jesus. Jesus is the pivot point of all human history. Before Him humanity lived under the Old Covenant, and now because Jesus came into the world we live under a New Covenant. History revolves around the person and work of Jesus Christ. In the big picture of redemptive history, the Old Covenant is passed away because Jesus has come.

The story of the Old Testament (the old covenant) is the story of even the best efforts, the best resolutions of God's people falling far short of God's perfect standard in His law. But the New Testament is a new covenant, sealed by the blood of Jesus on the cross, and it is not based on our obedience to the law. It is founded on Christ's obedience in our place. The new is come in Jesus.

For thousands of years, the Jewish people passed through a perpetual cycle of defeat, generation after generation. Whether a good king reigned over them or a bad king, whether they came from a good lineage or a bad lineage—over and over again Israel discovered their inability to save themselves by force of will or determination. At times they would even cry out in unison, 'We will keep the law of God, we and our children will commit to this!' Then soon afterwards they would yet again find themselves falling far short and wandering far off course.

In Christ, Paul informs us, that old way of failure has passed and the new way has come. Paul goes on to explain, a few verses later, the Christian gospel in the very simple terms of a great exchange: 'For our sake he made him to be sin who knew no sin, so that in him we might become the righteousness of God' (2 Cor. 5:21). Jesus took our sins, and their punishment, and gave us His righteousness.

Here is one of those pocket-sized jewels where the Christian message is summarized in a single verse, in a single sentence. On the cross, God made Jesus sin for us and gave us the righteousness of God in Jesus. Now, rather than striving to earn God's favor through obedience to His law, we by faith look to Jesus in whom we have God's own righteousness. *The righteousness of God!* This is not exaggeration: it is the better-than-can-be-imagined good news of Jesus. Those who trust in Jesus are, in God's eyes, as godly as Christ Himself. When God looks at believers, He does not see our continual failure: He sees the perfect obedience of His Son.

Intimately and Personally: the Old Way of Life Is Passed Away

When Paul speaks of the old having passed away, he is not merely speaking of the big-picture reality of the Old Testament giving way to the New Testament. He applies the work of Christ, not only historically, but intimately and personally: 'If anyone is in Christ, he is a new creation.' Clearly, Paul is not just speaking of the New Testament; he's talking about new people. He's talking about the New Testament becoming reality in the life of a believer.

Paul in 2 Corinthians 5:17 is referencing the Old Testament prophesies of Isaiah:

> *Behold,* I am doing a new thing; now it springs forth, do you not perceive it? I will make a way in the wilderness and rivers in the desert. (Isa. 43:19)

> For *behold,* I create new heavens and a new earth, and the former things shall not be remembered or come into mind. (Isa. 65:17)

If you are familiar with these words from Isaiah, you may have always thought of his prophecy in terms of a new heavens and earth that God will one day bring to pass when Jesus returns, after this world burns up. It is true there is a grand consummation event included in what Isaiah speaks of here. But don't miss the fact that Paul is quoting Isaiah in reference to the entire New Testament. There is a sense in which, in other words, the new creation is already begun: 'Behold, the new has come!'

The seeds of the new heavens and the new earth have already been planted because of what Jesus has done. 'If anyone is in Christ, he *is* a new creation'—not merely one day *will be* a new creation, not one day *will see* the new creation. Right now, if a person is in Christ by faith he or she *is* already a new creation.

What vivid, transcendent language! Jesus is not just another philosopher to add to the pile of philosophers. This is not even another biblical prophet who comes speaking in the name of God and with the words of God. No, Jesus is more than that. Jesus has established a new era by what He accomplished on the cross. He is making a river where before there was nothing but desert. He is making a new creation, even now.

For the one who becomes a Christian, the old worldview and the old way of life are passed away. The eyes are opened to beauties they never saw before, and disgust for sin is awakened where it did not exist before. The old self-consumed life is passed away.

Perhaps you have a dark past, full of things you—upon becoming a Christian—deeply regret. You can see sin was self-destructive and soul-afflicting. You were sin's slave, and sin was a hard master; you can still feel its scourge, bonds, and humiliation.

In Christ, you are a new creation! Your sins—past, present, and future—have been placed on Christ and punished in Christ. And you have been made 'the righteousness of God' in Christ.

Think about that! Take this in: in God's eyes, you are as righteous and good and pure as Christ Himself, because of

Jesus. If it were not true, it would be blasphemous to suggest such a thing! But because it is true, it is liberating and life-changing. Faith's acceptance of this reality is like the ex-slave who gradually comes to the realization that he or she is free. You can now walk upright; you don't have to flinch, or cower, or despair any longer.

Even as we embrace our new status in Christ, however, it does come with new opportunities and obligations as well. We are new creations in Christ, so the old things of our life are passed away. The new life has come, and so there will be a new way of life to match. There will be a freed man's life as a result of this emancipation Christ has accomplished on our behalf. The marks of our old heart, old lifestyle, and old priorities should be quickly fading, giving way to the newness of who we are in Christ. Paul speaks of this personal transformation, in the context of our new life: 'For the love of Christ controls us ... he died for all, that those who live might no longer live for themselves but for him who for their sake died and was raised' (2 Cor. 5:14-15).

Nowhere does Scripture suggest that God's grace in Christ allows us to continue in the very sins He died to save us from. If you died with Christ—if your sins were placed on Christ and punished in Christ—then you are raised with Christ to newness of life right here and now. When Christ rose, you rose with Him. This doesn't mean you don't still wrestle with it every morning as you get up and tell yourself yet again, 'I am free! I'm not a slave!' But it does mean your old ways are passed away and everything is new.

Christians Are Dying and Are Living

We, as new creatures, still have to struggle with our old nature every day. This is why it so important to continually soak our souls in the reality of the gospel message. We do not necessarily always feel the gospel truth, so we have to be continually reminded that it is true. The fact is, in the midst of the new life we have in Christ, we often feel as though we are dying.

Paul refers to this paradox in the chapter following his contention that 'behold, the new is come.' In 2 Corinthians 6:8-9, Paul writes, 'We are treated as impostors, and yet are true; as unknown, and yet well known; as dying, and *behold, we live...*'

If some preachers on television have perhaps given you the impression Christianity is an escape from poverty or difficulty (which in a way is a very exclusive kind of religion, isn't it, because if you're struggling with poverty or if you're struggling with difficulty, then you obviously don't fit into the club), Paul says nothing could be further from the truth. There is certainly an outward sense in which Christians are unknown, in which Christians are dying, in which Christians are afflicted, are sorrowful, are poor. If you look at Christianity around the globe you will find many, many Christians—who are loving God and serving Jesus—who live in the midst of tremendous struggles and difficulties, many times because of their faith.

Christianity is not a liberation from affliction or trial or difficulty. Christians know what it is to suffer, Christians know what it is to feel loss, to be betrayed, to experience deep regret, to struggle. But then, so does everyone else, don't they?

Even being rich doesn't mean you are exempt from pain or loss. All you have to do is read headlines about celebrities and it's obvious that there is a kind of poverty even while still rich. Being famous, popular, beautiful, or financially successful doesn't protect you from suffering.

What is different about Christians is not necessarily, Paul says, that we suffer. Suffering is universal in this broken and fallen world we live in. What is different about Christians is not *that* we suffer: it is *how* we suffer. We suffer in a different way. Our suffering is packed with purpose because our life, we have come to see, is packed with purpose. And our suffering, we are confident, has an end. The end is not annihilation, but a beautiful eternal bliss.

Therefore, our here-and-now sorrow is infused with comfort. It is pervaded with expectation. It is filled with joy. So Paul is able to go on in the same passage and describe Christians as 'sorrowful, yet always rejoicing; as poor, yet making many rich; as having nothing, yet possessing everything' (2 Cor. 6:10). Everything is new when you are in Christ, and one of the new things is how you deal with suffering. Even as you are suffering, even in the challenges and afflictions and ups and downs of life, there is life. We are dying and, behold, look just beneath the surface of our suffering. Yes, Christians are suffering just like everyone else; but beneath the suffering, there is the bedrock assurance Christians have in Jesus Christ that gives purpose and meaning and joy and life to even our dying.

Behold the living of Christians even in the midst of their dying. Behold our joy in the midst of our sorrow. Behold what we have even when we don't own anything. Behold what it means to be intimately known even when you're unknown, to be intimately loved and embraced by Jesus even when we may be unnoticed and unremarkable as far as worldly success is measured.

No one else may even care about what you are going through. But even while we're unknown, there is an incredibly wonderful, deep, and intimate way in which we are known, because God in Jesus knows us. And He knows what we're going through, He knows the difficulties we are facing. God knows the challenges that you are not only passing through but the pain they cause you.

Perhaps Christians, in some sense, are even experiencing more suffering than others because they are following Jesus and seeking to proclaim His name. Not everyone wants to hear that message, or be around someone who is living out its implications. There is often pushback. It is called persecution and many Christians experience it. Yet even as they suffer, there is a joy that none else can know or tell. As hymn writer Isaac Watts poetically expresses it,

The hill of Zion yields a thousand sacred sweets
Before we reach the heavenly fields or walk the golden streets.

Our hope as Christians is not just 'pie in the sky when we die.' For the Christian, there is right-now purpose, hope, and consolation. There are a thousand sacred sweets on which we are able to feast, to enjoy here and now because all things right now are becoming new! There is—even in the midst of our dying, even in the midst of our suffering—a beautiful living.

Again, don't get the wrong impression: all Christians have to be reminded and re-grounded in these realities on a regular basis. Living daily in light of eternity takes practice. As Jerry Bridges reminds us, you have to 'preach the gospel to yourself every day.' It doesn't come easily or naturally to anyone. This is nothing short of a supernatural perspective. And even though we, through faith, do experience real-time joy in the midst of suffering, it is also appropriate to long for a day when all suffering and all sin will be utterly eradicated. In fact, it would be wrong not to. The second coming of Christ is meant to be the great anchor on the other side of every Christian's life.

Paul unpacks this aspect of every Christian's hope in his first letter to Corinth. His great encouragement is, 'We shall be changed.'

> *Behold!* I tell you a mystery. We shall not all sleep, but we shall all be changed, in a moment, in the twinkling of an eye, at the last trumpet. For the trumpet will sound, and the dead will be raised imperishable, and we shall be changed. (1 Cor. 15:51-52)

Christian, this promise applies to you. If you are a believer in Jesus Christ, then one day you will be eternally and beautifully transformed. We have struggled with sin our whole lives—but we will be changed! No remnant of the traitorous rebel inside us, no residue of the wandering heart, no inkling of selfishness, not even the smallest yearning for pleasure or satisfaction or wisdom outside of Jesus.

You will go—not just a day, or a week, without any struggle with sin—you will go for years, hundreds of years, without any struggle with sin. Perhaps only then will it begin to really sink in: 'I have been changed.' Utterly, foundationally, beautifully changed!

All we have ever known is the inevitability of death—but we will be changed! Death will be dead, done away with. Instead of constantly feeling death's unavoidable approach, we will live through eternity in the realization that 'when we've been there 10,000 years, we've no less days to sing God's praise than when we first begun.'

We will live every moment in the knowledge that Jesus is our life, and that He is not going anywhere! We can never lose Him; we will never leave Him; and no one can, will, or will even want to separate us from Him ever again!

One day, dear Christian, we will have been changed ... and we will never be the same again. It is this knowledge that gives purpose and meaning to our life right now. Living forever with Christ, in sinless perfection, is what gives life to our dying now. There is a life that beats deep and strong underneath the death that Christians experience, the suffering that Christians experience. There is life because there is newness: a freedom from sin that we experience here and now, and a confident expectation that we will one day be changed completely.

Now Is the Favorable Time

Returning to the passage we began considering at the beginning of this chapter, let's look at the immediate context of Paul's statement in 2 Corinthians chapter 6. It is a little bit of a lengthy read, but Paul here repeats a single concept he wishes us to grasp. See if you pick up on his recurring theme.

In Christ God was reconciling the world to himself, not counting their trespasses against them, and entrusting to us the message of reconciliation. Therefore, we are ambassadors for Christ, God making his appeal through us. We implore you on behalf of Christ, be reconciled to God. For our sake he made him to be sin who knew no sin, so that in him we might become the righteousness of God. Working together with him, then, we appeal to you not to receive the grace of God in vain. For he says, 'In a favorable time I listened to you, and in a day of salvation I have helped you.' *Behold,* now is the favorable time; *behold,* now is the day of salvation. (2 Cor. 5:19-6:2)

One idea appears five times in this single passage: reconciliation. It's a beautiful word, isn't it? This is what Jesus was doing for us on the cross: reconciling former enemies. He was making peace between adversaries, bringing together opposing parties. God was, in Jesus Christ, reconciling us to Himself. He did this—as we've already considered—by making Jesus sin for us, who had never committed a single sin, and by giving us the righteousness of God in Jesus. Paul is speaking here, again, of both the big picture of redemptive history, and of the intimate and personal implications of this reality.

In the context of redemptive history, 'today' is the day of salvation. This is the age of the world of which Isaiah prophesied, that the Messiah would come and a new way would be made. A new creation would be brought to pass. There would be rivers running where there were deserts before. This is a new day. The new covenant in Jesus Christ has been revealed and the good news has been sent out—not just to Jews—but to the whole world!

We have the great blessing and privilege of living in the 'today' of the gospel!

What a shame to live in this marvelous age of the world, in which God's redemptive plan in Jesus Christ has been revealed, if we are then attracted to or distracted by lesser and temporary things. The apostle Peter, in one of his letters, informs us that the Old Testament prophets longed and labored to get even the smallest glimpses in Scripture of the coming Messiah. Meanwhile, you and I know who Jesus is and what He came to do on the cross. We get to open up our Bibles and read in the New Testament—the *New* Testament!—regarding the marvelous plan of God to save the world through Jesus Christ. We live in the 'today' of salvation. Not the looking forward to salvation, which is the Old Testament, but the today of salvation.

What a shame also then to live in this New Testament age, with the relevance of the gospel to every nation and language and pocket of the world, if we are not 'willing ambassadors,' as Paul says, for the reconciliation that is found in Christ! We have this mystery unpacked by divine revelation to us. But it is not merely for us. It is for the world.

This in turn brings us to the more intimate and personal application of this reality. Behold, not only is this the day of salvation as we look at redemptive history, but it can and should be the day of salvation for each and every person who hears and believes in Jesus' reconciling work. Now is the period in your life when you have been presented with this wonderful news. Considering, giving careful thought to, what God has done and is doing in Jesus Christ is not tomorrow's work. It is today's responsibility; it is today's opportunity for each of us individually. What will you do with it?

Behold! Linger and Consider:

- Have you previously thought of eternal life only as a future hope, or also as a present reality? How does here-and-now eternity influence our perspective?

- How has the old passed away, and the new already come—in the big picture of redemptive history, and in personal and more intimate ways?

- Christianity does not promise the removal of all our suffering. But it does provide joy in our sorrows. In what sense are Christians dying, and yet living?

- Why is *reconciliation* at the heart of the gospel message? How are we as sinners reconciled to the holy God who created us?

9 THE BLESSED WHO REMAIN STEADFAST

Job never saw why he suffered, but he saw God, and that was enough.
—Tim Keller

You may have seen the bumper sticker, 'Life is good.' There is certainly truth to that statement. Life is a blessing. It is an incredible privilege to exist, to be able to contribute a chapter to the human story and specifically to the great, overarching story of redemption. But it is also true that life doesn't always feel good. Nor is every life actually doing good, accomplishing a good purpose.

We often experience difficulties that are utterly outside our control and that make life hard. We also see our sinful behavior introducing destructive elements into our own life and the lives of others. It seems as though at times happiness is utterly out of our grasp, and life feels anything but good.

Into these real-life heart trials and sin struggles James speaks with profound sympathy and insight: '*Behold, we* consider those blessed who remained steadfast' (James 5:11). We consider them blessed as we raise our vision to greater purposes and joys than merely our momentary emotions. We consider them blessed as we raise our eyes to God, to His purposes, and to our opportunity to glorify Him in the midst of the mess of daily life.

Blessed are those who remain steadfast! 'Steadfastness' by its very nature includes suffering, struggle, effort ... but it also means not being conquered by those things. Everyone suffers, everyone faces challenges in life (some even of our own making), but blessed are those who endure.

James is not describing the simple, short-sighted success of merely muddling through trials without giving up. James is speaking of living a joyful, victorious life—in spite of personal failure and painful circumstances—by looking to and trusting in the good purposes and superior power of God who is working in and through us.

Steadfastness requires determination. It requires self-control even when we come to the realization many things are outside our control. This is why James, who begins his letter exhorting to steadfastness, spends a great deal of his letter considering things we can't control. Beholding things outside our control helps us look to the One who is in control.

Behold the Tongue

'Hold your tongue!' We might have heard our parents say this on countless occasions growing up. Yet we discover compliance to this command is not as easy as we might at first think. If we could hold our tongue, then many injuries and injustices could be avoided. But, though the tongue is small, James insists it is not easily controlled.

> Now if we put the bits into the horses' mouths so that they will obey us, we direct their entire body as well. *Behold* the ships also, though they are so great and are driven by strong winds, are still directed by a very small rudder wherever the will of the pilot directs. So also the tongue is a small part of the body, and yet it boasts of great things. *Behold* how great a forest is set aflame by such a small fire! And the tongue is a fire, a world of injustice. The tongue is set among our members, staining the entire body, and setting on fire the entire course of our life, and is set on fire by hell. (James 3:3-6)[1]

Just as a big horse is guided by a small bit, and a large ship is governed by a small rudder, and a huge fire is started by a small flame, the tongue has disproportionate power to do good or evil. And too often it is doing evil: in fact 'a world of injustice.' In the same way—just as these are small examples of big influences—'so also' is the tongue among our other body members.

As these small examples of big influences, just so is the tongue among our members. '*Our* members', James says. The apostle and brother of Jesus includes himself among those who have this affliction. But notice the flow here: the 'entire body' is stained by the tongue. Why? Because it inflames what is already in our nature; and this tongue-flame itself comes from hell, from something deeper and darker within us.

---

1   Author's translation.

James is famous for his bold, convicting rebukes regarding the use of our tongue. But it is important to see that James' discussion of the tongue is just one illustration of the many ways that we all offend God: 'We all stumble *in many ways*. And if anyone does not stumble in what he says, he is a perfect man, able also to bridle his whole body' (James 3:2).

According to James, our use of words is not the ultimate example of our sinfulness: it is just one example of the 'many ways' that we all frequently stumble. James wants us to consider the tongue so that we will, in doing so, come to realize the deeper sinful nature that underlies all of our sins.

The Untameable Tongue

This small tongue that has such a big effect should be easy to control, right? Just like the horse's bit, the ship's rudder, and the small flame. But we can't control our tongues! Why? Scottish theologian Sinclair Ferguson observes: '[The tongue] is so small. It has no bone. And yet it is so powerful to build up and destroy. Why does it do that? *Because it carries the breath of our souls into the world in which you live.*'[2]

The wickedness of the words we speak is the breath coming out of our souls; it is an expression of what is in our hearts. It is not just coincidence that our words are often cutting, or condescending, or gossip-spreading. Our hearts are corrupt, and so our words are corrupt. 'The tongue is ... setting on fire the entire course of our life, and is set on fire by hell.'

---

2   From Ferguson's Desiring God 2008 National Conference message: http://gospeltranslations.org/wiki/The_Tongue,_the_Bridle,_and_the_Blessing:_An_Exposition_of_James_3:1-12

In other words, the big problem is not just that we use our tongues the wrong way. This is merely the symptom of a deeper, darker issue. The tongue is set on fire by hell. When we speak corrupt words, we are merely giving vent to the hellish nature of our corrupt souls. Pride leads us to look down on others; envy causes us to undermine the success of others; bitterness causes us to resent others.

What we need, James is telling us, is not just a muzzle for our mouths. We need a cure for our souls.

THE PERFECT MAN

Truly, we all stumble in many ways. The wicked way we use our words is just one of many examples, James insists, of the depravity of our hearts. Thus, the answer for our tongue problem—as with the many other ways that we stumble and sin—is not, 'Clean up your act, and start using your words in better ways.' James pointedly insists that no one can tame his or her tongue (James 3:8). Just as no one can overcome any other sin, or their own sinful nature, in their own strength or by mere force of will.

Let's go back to verse 2: 'If anyone does not stumble in what he says, he is a perfect man, able also to bridle his whole body.' While many Bible students rush to say that 'perfect' here means 'mature,' is it possible that James actually had in mind a perfect man?

James, the brother of Jesus, had seen a perfect man. James had observed first-hand someone (Jesus!) who had never stumbled with a single word; James knew someone who had bridled His whole body.

James is convinced that, because we all stumble in many ways, none of us can bridle our tongue. But James is pointing us to the only 'perfect man' who has ever lived. He is our only hope, not only for overcoming sinful words, but for successfully bridling our sinful nature.

We all stumble in many ways, but Jesus did not stumble even in His use of words. We need this 'perfect man.'

Behold the Farmer

James continues, a few chapters later, with another example of a person who is out of control. You are not the only person who suffers from a lack of control. In fact, your lack of control inside displays a general principle around us. The entire world is—we have to confess—not revolving around us, is not performing according to our commands. James points us to the farmer, who is not in control either: 'Be patient, therefore...until the coming of the Lord. *Behold,* the farmer waits for the precious fruit of the earth, being patient over it until it receives the early and the late rain' (James 5:7, RSV).

Patience is one of the hardest lessons we are called to learn, isn't it? Remaining steadfast will mean enduring seasons of life that at times feel unbearably long. It would be one thing if the Lord would show us some clear path ahead and some action we could take toward that goal. But there are times when all we can do is watch and wait.

Perhaps you have been praying for a better work situation. You have sown job applications like seed; you have followed up with phone calls. You have agonized in prayer; you've done all you know to do. Now all you can do is wait.

John Milton wrote a beautiful poem expressing the difficulty of exercising patience. Sonnet 19 is a meditation on Milton's own blindness, and resulting feelings of inability to serve the Lord in any meaningful capacity. While Milton expresses his deep frustration and questions to God, he finally concludes, 'They also serve who only stand and wait.' Part of serving God is simply waiting on God. Waiting on His timing rather than trying to force our own, waiting on His plan rather than brashly moving forward with our own. They also serve who stand and wait ... and wait and wait and wait. The farmer is serving, not only when he is plowing. He is wise not only when he is working, but when he is waiting. He waits for the rain he needs in order for the harvest to be fruitful, the rain that he himself cannot bring.

We do not have to share the agricultural surroundings of James to learn the lesson he is teaching. The farmer in reality is of course one example of what every human has to do at different points in life. We are called to trust God in circumstances over which we have no control.

Like the farmer, we all have to wait on God's timing for things outside our own control, for future fruit from our labors ... and ultimately for the coming of the Lord. It is not enough to wait for a painful trial to end, or some big prayer request to be answered. There will always be another one coming soon. Ultimately, we are waiting for the Lord to come back! That may be after we die, so we are in this for the long haul.

How do we hang in there for a lifetime of suffering? Notice the motivation James provided from the outset, 'Be patient, therefore ... until the coming of the Lord.'

Behold the Judge

James opened his letter with an exhortation to suffering saints to remain steadfast. He warned them against pervasive sin that seeks to ignite forest fires of trouble. He encouraged them with the example of the farmer, who works hard and then waits long. James then provides the foundational hope that makes all this suffering and sin-fighting and waiting worth it. '*Behold,* the Judge is standing at the door' (James 5:9).

Ultimately, we are not waiting for the end of a trial, or for the answer to a prayer. We are not merely concerned about some short-term success; we are not just waiting for things outside our control to settle down. When we are thinking correctly and emoting accurately, what we are truly waiting for is the coming of the Lord. Behold, the Judge of the universe: He controls everything!

In the immediate context, James is reminding his readers that the Judge is standing at the door—His return imminent—because his readers are wrestling with the reality of their own sin and the sins of others: 'Do not grumble against one another, brothers, so that you may not be judged; *behold,* the Judge is standing at the door' (James 5:9).

Here is a poignant reminder. True to reality, a significant portion of our patient endurance will involve patiently enduring our own sin struggles as well as the sins of others that directly affect us. Yet before you grumble at, or judge, others—remember that your own Judge is standing at the door. Your being longsuffering toward others will seem like nothing once you yourself are standing in front of the Creator of the universe to give an account! Our soon-coming appearance before the Judge of the world should warn us to sober, humble endurance even with difficult and harmful people.

The coming of the Judge, however, is not only a warning: it is also the sweet consummation of everything we've been hoping for and looking toward. In the verse immediately preceding James' warning that the Judge is at the door, he expresses the same reality in comforting terms: 'Be patient. Establish your hearts, for the coming of the Lord is at hand' (James 5:8). Jesus is not only coming as the great Judge of sin, but also as the Lord who has been benevolently directing every step, every detail of our lives for our good and His glory.

Thus, just a few verses later, we read the remarkable statement with which we began this chapter. '*Behold*, we consider those blessed who remained steadfast. You have heard of the steadfastness of Job, and you have seen the purpose of the Lord, how the Lord is compassionate and merciful' (James 5:11).

It is absolutely vital for us to trust the goodness and love of God toward us in the midst of all our sin struggles and patient endurance of things outside our control. We must trust that God has good purposes for the difficult things He allows in our lives. Even when we can't see why we are suffering, if we see God in our suffering that will be enough.

James points us to Job. As the tongue is just one example of the failures of our sinful nature, Job is just one example of a person who suffered patiently, struggled with sin failures, and yet was brought through faith in God to a happy end.

Job is a wonderful example who remained steadfast and was blessed. But there are many others to whom we could also point. Ruth labored patiently and faithfully through personal loss, singleness, and poverty; and in the end she saw God's good purposes for her come to fruition. Joseph endured personal betrayal and slander, and then saw God work it all together for his good and the good of his family. Paul was in prison for preaching the gospel, with other Christians actually trying to add affliction to his bonds, yet he found God's grace sufficient for the trial and so was brought to rejoice in the Lord. Each of these men and women of faith looked to God and so received the strength they needed to suffer well, to remain steadfast.

Jesus Himself is our definitive example of patient suffering. We are told in Hebrews 12:2 to look to 'the founder and perfecter of our faith, who for the joy that was set before him endured the cross, despising the shame, and is seated at the right hand of the throne of God.' We consider those blessed who remain steadfast, and Jesus is the ultimate reminder of this reality. Jesus perfectly fulfills the promise James provides for everyone who patiently endures: 'Blessed is the man who remains steadfast under trial, for when he has stood the test he will receive the crown of life, which God has promised to those who love him' (James 1:12).

The great comfort and encouragement for every believer is that Jesus Himself is standing at the door. His return is imminent, and those who remain steadfast will soon join Him in receiving the crown of life, and experience complete victory over every struggle they have endured in this world. This reality is sometimes difficult to see when we are surrounded by suffering or enduring a lengthy season of waiting. But, behold, we consider those blessed who remain steadfast.

Behold! Linger and Consider:

- Life is good, but life is also hard. How does James encourage us in the hardness?

- How does our untameable tongue drive us to Jesus Christ as our only hope?

- Waiting does not always feel productive. What can a farmer teach us about patience, about dependence on God?

- The fact that Jesus is coming again soon brings both conviction and comfort. How does James draw out both these lessons from Jesus' imminent return?

10 HE IS COMING

To be united with that Life in the eternal Sonship of Christ is,
strictly speaking, the only thing worth a moment's consideration.
—C.S. Lewis

We noticed at the beginning of this book that the New Testament opens with more than ten occurrences of the command to 'behold' as the story of Jesus Christ's birth is narrated. Now the New Testament closes with no less than thirty cries to 'behold' in the book of Revelation alone!

At the very outset of the Revelation, we as readers are called to, '*Behold,* he is coming with the clouds, and every eye will see him' (Rev. 1:7). Jesus is extolled in the preceding verses in terms of the great redemption He has accomplished for every believer—He loves us, He has freed us from our sins, and He has made us into a kingdom whose one common ground is Jesus. But we are immediately reminded the emphasis is not on us, but on the fact that such a glorious redemption means that all glory and power belong to Him: 'Behold, he is coming...'

In Revelation, gone forever is the humiliation of Jesus the Christ. No more is Jesus a lowly baby in a trough, or an unknown carpenter's son, or even a great teacher who is submitted to earthly authorities. Jesus is no longer the suffering servant or the silent lamb before His shearers. Yes, Jesus is still the Lamb in the book of Revelation, but now and forever the Lamb is on the throne!

In the book of Revelation, Jesus is 'the Alpha and the Omega'—the One who created everything in the beginning for His pleasure, and the one who now is drawing all creation to its conclusion. In the book of Revelation, Jesus is 'the Almighty'—there will be resistance at the end, but resistance is futile because all power belongs to Jesus! Even the two horrible beasts that appear in Revelation 13 and 14 are only 'given' power and 'allowed' to exercise limited authority for a specific period of time.

In the Revelation, we are told to 'behold,' to consider this Jesus now, because 'he is coming ... and every eye will see him' whether we want to or not, whether we look for Him or not, whether we reject Him or not. As C.S. Lewis well expresses, we can no more diminish this divine glory by refusing to worship Him than a lunatic can put out the sun by scribbling the word 'darkness' on the walls of his cell.

An old preacher once defined the theme of the book of Revelation as 'Jesus wins!' That's true. But perhaps even better we might sum it up with these two words repeated in Revelation: 'Worship God!' (Rev. 19:10; 22:9)—because here Jesus is shown to be God, and the point of the book is our response to Him as God.

That's it. If you get that, you understand Revelation. You don't have to be a degreed theologian or a code-cracking mathematician. You just need to know this: the Word of God says Jesus wins because Jesus is God, and so we are to worship Him. If you keep that fact in mind, then all of the other facts fall into place.

And so we are called in the book of Revelation to behold Jesus in all His resplendent, transcendent glory. Behold Jesus, who is sovereign over death and life, over hell and heaven, over the now and the evermore.

Jesus Has the Keys of Death and Hades

The book opens with Jesus' majesty from the outset. He is the triumphant and regal Christ, the Son of God. In Revelation 1:10-18 Jesus is described in apocryphal terms as having a loud voice like a trumpet or a great waterfall, and being clothed in royal apparel. His hair is white as snow, his eyes like fire, his feet like polished brass; and He holds seven angels in His hand. From His mouth protrudes a sword, and His whole countenance is brighter than the sun in the Middle East at noon!

Pause and take in that composite picture. No matter how many times you may have read this depiction of Jesus before, it is genuinely awesome—producing a mixture of reverence and wonder. This description is meant to bombard our senses: our eyes dazzled by His brilliance, our ears stunned by His splendor, our whole being trembling at His approach.

We dare not, as we go through the book of Revelation, take such resplendent language lightly, because the fact is these are merely inadequate attempts to describe the reality of Jesus in all His real and present glory. One day every eye will see Him, not merely read a description of Him. Every knee will bow before Him, whether voluntarily and joyfully, or involuntarily and reluctantly. There is no arguing with total authority; there is no protesting against omnipotence. The picture of Jesus that John here provides us is meant to prepare us for the day when we will see Jesus with our own eyes.

It is interesting—and should be instructive—that although centuries have passed since John Newton wrote *Amazing Grace*, life is still limited and death is still certain. The space age and the smart phone, while certainly changing our lives, have not unbound them. We can still sing with personal conviction that 'this flesh and heart shall fail, and mortal life shall cease.' Which should in turn remind us that the truths Newton wrote about were not merely personal or subjective feelings, but eternal realities.

For every human being, there is a limited number of seasons we will see, of opportunities we will have. And then this mortal life shall cease. The reality of death, and of the failing of mind and body which most of us will experience years prior to death, should change the way we look at life. We must live for things that will outlast us, and other failing human forms.

On the other hand, it is comforting to realize that the challenges and trials of this life are not eternal either. For every Christian, sorrow and pain will die along with their body. When their flesh and heart fails, so will the ability of this sin-cursed world to bother them any longer. This was comforting to an ex-slave-trader with many regrets, who also suffered in many ways physically. As long as life persists, pain persists; but once this mortal life ceases, so will the grief. Then, and only then, 'I shall possess... a life of joy and peace.'

John tells us of his own encounter with the resurrected and glorified Jesus in order to prepare us for our inevitable and quickly-approaching confrontation with the Lord.

> When I saw him, I fell at his feet as though dead. But he laid his right hand on me, saying, 'Fear not, I am the first and the last, and the living one. I died, and *behold* I am alive forevermore, and I have the keys of Death and Hades.' (Rev. 1:17-18)

God became human! He was born from a virgin as the God-man named Jesus. He lived a perfect life for thirty-three years, then submitted to an excruciating death on a Roman cross in order to take the place of sinners. But then He rose from the dead and appeared to over 500 witnesses in order to publicly display that death did not conquer Him. Jesus conquered death for every believer who will ever live!

Jesus has the keys to death and beyond. That's all we need to know to be awestruck as mere mortals. Jesus has the keys to what no doctor has ever been able to cure, no scientist has ever been able to accomplish. Jesus has complete authority over everlasting life and eternal death.

Jesus' absolute power, though sobering for anyone to consider, is meant to be a great comfort to believers in Christ, who will often suffer persecution. Because the world hated the Master, the world will also hate His disciples. We see this demonic opposition, and the mastery of Jesus over it, just a chapter later as Jesus speaks to the churches in Asia:

> Do not fear what you are about to suffer. *Behold,* the devil is about to throw some of you into prison, that you may be tested ... Be faithful unto death, and I will give you the crown of life. (Rev. 2:10)

Christian, you may face many sorrows and losses in this world. Jesus does not ignore the pains and difficulties of your life. But Jesus is waiting on the other end to welcome you with a crown of everlasting life.

Be in awe, not of the great persecutions that come against you as a Christian, the great trials that you face as a Christian. Be in awe of the One who is in control of those persecutions and difficulties and pains that you face. Be in awe of Jesus who has the keys to death and to Hades.

Jesus Has Prevailed to Open the Book of Unfolding History

While backpacking through Europe many years ago, I was able to take a tour of the Palace of Versailles, near Paris, the royal residence of King Louis XIV. The building and grounds are now valued at over $50 billion. The expanse of the gardens and the magnitude of the palace itself made me—in my dirty, worn hiking gear—feel at once greatly impressed and greatly out of place.

Amazingly, however, when John receives a vision of the throne room in heaven itself—in chapters four and five of Revelation—he is welcomed and even invited in.

> After this I looked, and *behold,* a door standing open in heaven! And the first voice, which I had heard speaking to me like a trumpet, said, 'Come up here, and I will show you what must take place after this.' At once I was in the Spirit, and *behold,* a throne stood in heaven, with one seated on the throne. (Rev. 4:1-2)

Though John certainly feels his own smallness, it is not because of the opulence surrounding him but because the Son of God sits on the throne and wields His infinite power for the good of His people. Jesus the Lamb is alone glorious, alone qualified to stand at the helm of history.

John sees, in his vision, a scroll that is sealed with seven seals. These seven seals reflect the importance of its contents. Yet no one in heaven or on earth is able to open the seals and to read the scroll. Not even the mighty angel who serves as John's tour guide in the vision is worthy to open this scroll. John begins to weep in his vision. Then John is comforted by these words: 'Weep no more; *behold,* the Lion of the tribe of Judah, the Root of David, has conquered, so that he can open the scroll and its seven seals' (Rev. 5:5).

As the seven seals of this scroll are progressively opened in the following chapters, we discover it contains the unfolding events of human history—including the irrepressible, overwhelming judgments of God. We are reminded of the cosmic dimensions of Jesus' rule. There is *nothing* that is *not* under His power and authority! The leadership of nations, the movements of terrorists, the activities of nature are all under Jesus' control, and are ultimately answerable to Jesus.

We must also apply this cosmic lesson on a personal level, however, as we see the repeated exhortations in Revelation for each believer to overcome through perseverance. We ought always to have in mind that Jesus is sovereign, not only over the great events of the world but also over the details of our daily life. Every decision, every challenge, every motivation is to be submitted to the One who sits on the throne and holds the scroll of human history in His hand.

We are often tempted, I think, to try to take this scroll and open it ourselves. We seek to map out our entire future, or we attempt to control people and circumstances in order to reach our own desired outcomes. Or we struggle with the very opposite and feel helpless like John to think of a world that is out of control—we weep with guilt over the past, or anxiety about the future. All the while, regardless of our efforts or emotions, only Jesus the Lamb of God is able and worthy to hold the scroll of unfolding history.

Included in this section of the Revelation is the glorious scene of the redeemed people of God offering praise to the Lamb of God. God's people are a global people, hailing from points all over the world and from every age of the earth. They are diverse in their ethnicity, their language, their cultural backgrounds.

> After this I looked, and *behold,* a great multitude that no one could number, from every nation, from all tribes and peoples and languages, standing before the throne and before the Lamb, clothed in white robes, with palm branches in their hands, and crying out with a loud voice, 'Salvation belongs to our God who sits on the throne, and to the Lamb!' (Rev. 7:9-10)

This is a majestic scene, an impressive scene. But the pressing question to ask, as we behold this scene, is: am I one of the people in that crowd? Am I clothed in the white robes of Jesus' salvation, or am I planning to stand before the great white throne wearing only the dirty rags of my own best efforts?

Jesus is the Lion of the tribe of Judah; He is the Lamb of God who is uniquely qualified to hold the scroll of unfolding history, including the unfolding story of our own lives individually. In all the ups and downs of life, the song on our lips ought therefore to constantly be, 'Salvation belongs to our God.'

Jesus Is the Faithful and True King of Kings

We often think of 'judgment' as being a bad thing. When we read of judgment in the Bible the idea automatically has a negative and unsettling connotation to us. We think it is wrong for others to judge us, and we definitely don't like the idea of God judging us. But this is a wrong way of thinking about judgment. Good and just judgment involves setting the record straight, and meting out appropriate commendation as well as condemnation. In reality, the righteous judgment of God on a sinful world ought to be something we long to see— when every wrong will finally be made right. No one will, in the end, get away with evil.

Think of judgment, in other words, in terms of the parable Jesus tells of the widow who comes begging resolutely for judgment.[1] She refuses to be turned away, because she so

---

1   This parable is found in Luke 18:1-8.

desperately wants justice to be served. She longs to see a king judge her case, and take up for her in her affliction. This is because good judgment puts everything right, puts everything the way it is supposed to be.

In chapters 17 to 19 of the Revelation, we read about the judgment of the prostitute of Babylon, who killed so many Christians:

> After this I heard what seemed to be the loud voice of a great multitude in heaven, crying out, 'Hallelujah! Salvation and glory and power belong to our God, for his judgments are true and just; for he has judged the great prostitute who corrupted the earth with her immorality, and has avenged on her the blood of his servants.' (Rev. 19:1-2)

Regardless of who Babylon may specifically be or represent here, we can say with certainty that what is true of—and applies to—Babylon in this passage also applies to every group of people, in every age of the world, who has systematically sought to exterminate the witness of Christ in the world.

Several years ago, as the terrorist group ISIS was hacking its horrible way through the Middle East, I received a prayer request from a Christian missionary team who was in Iraq. It read in part:

> We lost the city of Qaraqosh ... This is the city we have been smuggling food to. ISIS has pushed back Peshmerga (Kurdish forces) and is within 10 minutes of where our team is working. Thousands more fled into the city of Erbil last night. The UN evacuated its staff in Erbil. Our team is unmoved and will stay. Prayer is needed!

What gives Christians the courage to stay and to stand for Christ when the United Nations is on the run? (Or, perhaps just as difficult, to remain in the region laboring toward restoration for years afterward, as this particular missionary team did?) It is rock-solid faith in this reality: salvation, and glory, and power belong to Jesus alone. His judgments are, and will be, true and righteous. Everyone who has ever spilled the blood of innocent people will either be judged themselves, or their sin will be judged in Jesus when they come to faith in Christ!

Thus, we read what is perhaps the climax of the victorious portrayal of Jesus Christ, in Revelation 19:

> Then I saw heaven opened, and *behold,* a white horse! The one sitting on it is called Faithful and True, and in righteousness he judges and makes war. His eyes are like a flame of fire, and on his head are many diadems, and he has a name written that no one knows but himself. He is clothed in a robe dipped in blood, and the name by which he is called is The Word of God ... On his robe and on his thigh he has a name written, King of kings and Lord of lords. (Rev. 19:11-13, 16)

If you have not yet seen Jesus as the faithful and true Judge of the world, as the King of kings and Lord of lords—then you have not yet seen Jesus. But, behold! Jesus is coming and every eye will see Him on that day, in all His glory and in all His justice.

Jesus Is Making All Things New

In Revelation 20 we witness the binding of Satan and the reigning of the saints with Christ for a thousand years—all vividly described in apocryphal language. At the end of the thousand years, Satan is released and seeks to deceive the nations and to gather an army to himself. However, this satanic army—whose purpose is to make war against Jesus—is devoured by fire that God sends from heaven. Satan's desperate and despicable rebellion ends in utter defeat.

Then we read in Revelation 20:10, 'And the devil who had deceived them was thrown into the lake of fire and sulfur where the beast and the false prophet were, and they will be tormented day and night forever and ever.' Never forget that hell is not the devil's hell. Satan is not ruling hell: he is an inmate there. Hell is Jesus' hell: He holds the keys to the lake of fire.

Following Satan's judgment, every human in history is judged by Jesus, and anyone not found written in the Book of Life is cast into the lake of fire along with the devil and his angels.

And so, we read in Revelation 21 and 22 that Jesus brings about a new heavens and a new earth—and this shouldn't surprise us—this new heavens and earth is all about Jesus (the way this earth should be). Jesus is the temple, the place of worship, in the new heavens and earth. Jesus is the light of this new and perfect world, so there is no need for a sun. The description of Jesus' glory is majestic; but perhaps most striking of all is the fact that this King of all kings does not sit in His palace in heaven, separate from His human creatures. Jesus is not Louis XIV. For all eternity, Jesus lives among us.

> '*Behold,* the dwelling place of God is with man. He will dwell with them, and they will be his people, and God himself will be with them as their God. He will wipe away every tear from their eyes, and death shall be no more, neither shall there be mourning, nor crying, nor pain anymore, for the former things have passed away.' And he who was seated on the throne said, '*Behold,* I am making all things new.' Also he said, 'Write this down, for these words are trustworthy and true.' (Rev. 21:3-5)

Here is the greatest promise of all: God not only became human, in the person of Jesus, but God will forever live with us. No more separation. No more waiting. This is the consummation of all God has planned for this old sin-cursed world, and every future moment for the people of God will be spent in the presence of God.

This is the magnificent expectation of every believer, to be forever with the Lord. What comfort these words bring to the heart of each one who has long anticipated the personal presence of their Savior!

John goes on to record the very words of Jesus, as He sits on His throne in heaven, '*Behold,* I am making all things new' (Rev. 21:5). Jesus promises to give water, without charge, to those who are thirsty; He promises that those who overcome will be His children and will receive the new earth as their inheritance.

In this world, sin has reigned in every era of human history. But, behold, Jesus is making everything new! This earth is full of pain, and loss, and confusion. But, behold, God has come to live with broken humanity and He will wipe away every tear, and there will be no more death or sorrow or pain! In this world godly acts of service are often performed without much notice or reward; and wicked deeds often seem to go unpunished. But, behold, when Jesus makes everything new believers will inherit all things, and those not in Christ will be righteously judged for their wicked acts.

Jesus Is Coming Again Soon

Jesus is right now seated at God's right hand. But His ministry has not ceased, nor is He merely waiting until He returns to earth. Christ's present ministry includes preparing a place for believers (John 14:2-3). That alone is breathtaking to consider! It took only six days to create this entire universe—what must our heavenly accommodations be like, which Jesus has been preparing for 2,000 years!

Jesus is also engaged in on-going, empathetic mediation for His children. When we sin, therefore, we have an advocate with the Father, Jesus Christ the righteous (1 John 2:1). The very one who paid for our sins, and who has given us His perfect righteousness through faith, is advocating for us in heaven! No wonder the writer of Hebrews exhorts us to 'come boldly' to the throne of grace (Heb. 4:16)! We enter a throne room that is occupied by the very one who has paid for our sins, who is touched by our weakness.

In answer to the needs of His people, Jesus has 'poured out' the Holy Spirit—with all His comforting, sustaining, guiding power and wisdom—among His people (Acts 2:33). Jesus promised that the presence of the Spirit with us would be superior even to Jesus' own physical presence with us (John 16:7).

Yet, with all this labor taking place there is also a certain anticipation permeating heaven. Whether we on earth recognize it or not, there is a day approaching. It is the end of all days, the day of the Lord, in which every knee will bow and every tongue will confess that Jesus Christ is Lord. Jesus must reign until He has put all His enemies under his feet (1 Cor. 15:25).

There are many descriptions of the second coming of Christ, and all of them are impressive. We are told that the earth and heavens will in that day be burned up (2 Pet. 3:10). We know the dead will rise from the grave to be judged. But most important of all, we know that Jesus Himself will return from heaven.

Jesus announced this urgently in the beginning of the Revelation: '*Behold,* I am coming quickly!' (Rev. 3:11, NASB). We are again warned in the middle of the action of John's revelation, '*Behold,* I am coming like a thief! Blessed is the one who stays awake...' (Rev. 16:15). And, finally, at the conclusion of the book, we are once again reminded, in rapid-fire succession, of the imminent return of Jesus:

And *behold,* I am coming soon. Blessed is the one who keeps the words of the prophecy of this book ... *Behold,* I am coming soon, bringing my recompense with me, to repay each one for what he has done. I am the Alpha and the Omega, the first and the last, the beginning and the end. (Rev. 22:7, 12-13)

There is only one proper response from every believer to the soon-coming Savior. It is the same enraptured reply we hear from John's lips, 'Amen. Come, Lord Jesus!'

Jesus is returning soon! Behold, when He comes every eye will see Him. But *how* will you see Him in that day? As restorer, comforter, and redeemer? Behold Jesus now by faith, so that when you see Him with your own eyes you can joyfully embrace Him.

Behold! Linger and Consider:

- We often tend to think of Jesus as the baby in the manger, or as the suffering servant. But how does Revelation depict Jesus?

- We don't like to think about death, but we all need to. What does it mean for Jesus to have the keys of death?

- How does it change our perspective to consider Jesus as King of kings? How should it influence our politics, or how we respond to persecution?

- What are some things you look forward to seeing made 'new'? What does the Bible hold out as the greatest promise of the new heavens and earth?

- How should the imminent return of Jesus shape our view of the present? The future?

CONCLUSION

Worship is a believer's response to God's revelation of Himself.
It is expressing wonder, awe, and gratitude for the worthiness,
the greatness, and the goodness of our Lord.
—Nancy Leigh DeMoss

We huddled together in a small, chilly room in Siberia. I was supposed to have been speaking at a 'pastors' conference,' but due to weather and other factors only a handful of men had made it. Eventually every pastor around the table (including the pastor from the coldest inhabited region on earth) admitted they were thinking about quitting the ministry.

Seriously.

Like, today.

I expected our host to pipe in with encouraging words. But no. He admitted he was considering throwing in the towel as well. And me? I had just landed after dealing with some of the most painful and challenging pastoral issues I'd ever faced back home. I admitted to the others that I felt beat down and ready to give up.

Then something beautiful happened. We prayed together, with lots of tears. And then one at a time we began reminding each other of the reality of who God is for us, in Jesus. I don't know if it was just me, but it felt like the room got warmer as we preached the gospel to each other in hushed tones and were reminded that we were family, and that God is our Father.

Pastors—like all Christians—sometimes lose sight of the glory and wonder of what we ourselves are believing, counseling, and proclaiming. When our problems loom large in our vision, then God can appear small and insignificant.

This is one of the many reasons the divine imperative to *behold* is so timely and so needed for us all. We do not by nature gaze by faith at the big and eternal things. We are too often instead transfixed in fear or despair by the realities we see surrounding us every day. The temporary and physical pushes out the eternal and spiritual, if we are not careful.

Knowing our propensity to fasten our attention on the wrong things, God has not only given us His Word, the Bible, but He repeatedly calls us to snap out of our sin-stupor and fixate on the glory of who God is and what He is doing in and through Jesus Christ.

The command to *behold* appears hundreds of times in the New Testament alone. Why? Because the truths revealed in God's Word are genuinely gaze-worthy. And because Jesus Christ, who is the great subject matter of the whole Bible, is truly awesome in His divine person and work.

Conclusion

Throughout this book, we have attempted to consider some of the truths, some of the occasions, some of the people that the Bible tells us specifically to 'Behold.' We want to refocus the affections of each reader on these eternal realities that have the power to save us from our own mundane solutions, and satisfy our glory-hunger as we feast on Jesus. Utilizing the Bible's admiration of its own content—specifically its repeated imperative to 'Behold' the wonderful truths and events it is proclaiming—our goal has been to walk through the New Testament in a way that ignites holy wonder in each of our hearts.

We have considered the birth, death, resurrection, and return of Jesus; and we have touched on such practical matters as discipleship, personal holiness, and perseverance. But of course we have just scratched the surface; the ocean depths of God's Word await your own further personal study.

The word *behold,* by the way, is not the only often-missed treasure in God's Word. If you look closely you will find similarly small, underestimated, underutilized windows into the glory of God's redemptive story. For example, you might be greatly blessed by a brief word study of 'Selah,' which we find repeated in the Psalms. Or take time to contemplate the significance of Jesus—who cannot lie—prefacing so many of His statements with, 'Truly, truly.'

To be clear, there is nothing magic about the word 'behold.' It is not a key to some mysterious Bible code. But the word is meaningful, as is every word of Scripture. It's my hope that this brief work has piqued your interest, and will enliven your personal Bible reading for years to come. When you read your Bible on your own, and you come across the command to *behold,* I pray that from now on you are receptive to that instruction.

It is an invitation to glory. It is like a marker for a scenic lookout: encouraging you to pause, to consider afresh the wonder of what God Himself has put in front of your eyes.

Though we have focused chiefly on the New Testament imperatives to 'behold,' we find another (and very instructive) occurrence of the same concept in the Psalms. David writes, 'One thing have I asked of the LORD, that will I seek after ... *to gaze upon the beauty of the LORD ...*' (Ps. 27:4).

When you think of a 'practical' book, or sermon, or podcast, what potential subject matters come to mind? A discussion about personal finances? Or some hints for overcoming discouragement? Perhaps a 'how to' on personal devotion time? Maybe even a message calling for charitable work?

These things certainly are practical, but the psalmist David joins the chorus of New Testament witnesses in order to remind us that the most practical thing we can do is gaze by faith at the glory of God in Christ, until we are once again ravished with the beauty of the Lord. This is the 'one thing' we are seeking to do in this book, and in all of life.

The hymnwriter Helen Lemmel beautifully expresses this singular pursuit:

> *Turn your eyes upon Jesus,*
> *Look full in His wonderful face,*
> *And the things of earth will grow strangely dim,*
> *In the light of His glory and grace.*

Also available from Christian Focus Publications...

Forewords by Dr. Michael Reeves and Daryl Heald

BIG
HEARTED

*Are You Giving Happily
or Hesitantly?*

JOEL MORRIS

ISBN 978-1-5271-0698-7

Big Hearted

Are You Giving Happily or Hesitantly?

Joel Morris

Every Christian is called to give – of our money, our time, our talents – but how often do we give just because we feel we should? We resent the sacrifice of things we could enjoy ourselves, and the biblical idea of giving cheerfully seems almost impossible. Or we give because we know that it will make us feel good. Or because we want other people to think well of us. But this is not godly giving.

The motivation behind our giving is important. Giving, like everything else in the Christian life, begins with the two greatest commandments – to love the Lord our God with everything we have, and to love our neighbour as ourselves. Our cheerful, outrageous and extravagant generosity begins with unreservedly loving the God who has freely given us all things.

The love of God spills out of the pages of Big Hearted. Joel Morris' beautiful work will inspire you to ask God to conform you into His image – namely that of a cheerful, sacrificial, generous, loving, and big–hearted giver. Read, apply, and rejoice.

Chuck Bentley
CEO, Crown.org & Author, *7 Gray Swans, Trends That Impact Our Financial Future*

Christian Focus Publications

Our mission statement —

STAYING FAITHFUL
In dependence upon God we seek to impact the world
through literature faithful to His infallible Word, the Bible.
Our aim is to ensure that the Lord Jesus Christ is presented as
the only hope to obtain forgiveness of sin, live a useful life and
look forward to heaven with Him.

Our books are published in four imprints:

CHRISTIAN
FOCUS

Popular works including biographies, commentaries, basic doctrine
and Christian living.

CHRISTIAN
HERITAGE

Books representing some of the
best material from the rich heritage
of the church.

MENTOR

Books written at a level suitable
for Bible College and seminary
students, pastors, and other serious
readers. The imprint includes
commentaries, doctrinal studies,
examination of current issues and
church history.

CF4•K

Children's books for quality Bible
teaching and for all age groups: Sunday
school curriculum, puzzle and activity
books; personal and family devotional
titles, biographies and inspirational stories — because you are never too young
to know Jesus!

Christian Focus Publications Ltd,
Geanies House, Fearn, Ross-shire,
IV20 1TW, Scotland, United Kingdom.
www.christianfocus.com